Software Evolution

SOFTWARE EVOLUTION

THE SOFTWARE MAINTENANCE CHALLENGE

Lowell Jay Arthur

A Wiley-Interscience Publication

JOHN WILEY & SONS

New York / **Chichester** / **Brisbane** / **Toronto** / **Singapore**

Copyright © 1988 by John Wiley & Sons, Inc.

Library of Congress Cataloging in Publication Data:

Arthur, Lowell Jay, 1951-
  Software evolution.

  "A Wiley-Interscience publication."
  Bibliography: p.
  1. Software maintenance   I. Title.

QA76.76.S64A78   1987   005.1'6   87-20972
ISBN 0-471-62871-9

Printed in the United States of America

10 9 8 7 6 5 4 3

To Tom Prieve,
Many thanks

Preface

In the software community the word "maintenance" has acquired a deadly negative connotation. An ugly word, "maintenance." It seems to imply that there is something desperately wrong with a software product (it must be someone's fault) and that the workers who slave over it are nothing more than blue-collar mechanics.

That's why this book is dedicated to software "evolution." As businesses grow, software must grow. As technology improves, software must evolve to match the technology. Every system—government, business, or personal—is in a constant state of flux, changing, growing. Software must *evolve* to meet the growing needs of these complex organizations and of people.

Software maintenance has been evolving at the same time as software. The five stages of maintenance maturity have been described as: chaos, concern, methodology, measurement, and control. This book will help you establish a repeatable maintenance process. You've probably already experienced chaos and concern. I also speak briefly about measurement. I developed these thoughts more fully in *Measuring Programmer Productivity and Software Quality,* published by Wiley, 1985. Somehow, I put the cart before the horse. Having the sort of quality control that delivers high-quality software productively is still a distant goal for most organizations. This book will help you reach the third level of maintenance maturity—a productive, high-quality, maintenance process.

Actually most software maintainers are involved in software evolution, not maintenance. In a typical software maintenance environment, corrective maintenance (fixing defects) consumes less than 10% of all resources. The rest focus on software evolution.

The software evolution process is shown in Figure 1. Evolution begins with a request for change and ends with the release of a software product.

As shown in the center of the figure, this book describes three types of maintenance: corrective (fixing software), adaptive (enhancing software), and one you may not have thought of, perfective (improving software quality). These are identical to the functions of an automobile mechanic: they fix problems, add radial tires or performance equipment, and change the oil or tune up the engine. Software maintainers often perform the first two but forget to take time out to fine-tune the software to prevent defects or to make it easier to enhance. Doing all three types *well* is essential to successful software evolution.

This book will describe what you need to do to establish a healthy, effective, evolutionary environment for supporting existing systems. Some of the key items are change control, system releases, configuration management, and software-maintenance management.

Chapters 7 and 8 will cover every aspect of perfective maintenance, from choosing software candidates to reengineering the software to improve its quality. These two chapters can teach maintainers and developers a lot about keeping software on the evolutionary ladder.

There is a method to this book's madness. It discusses the software-maintenance process in chronological order. Chapter 2 talks about entering a request for change, and Chapter 10 covers releasing the finished

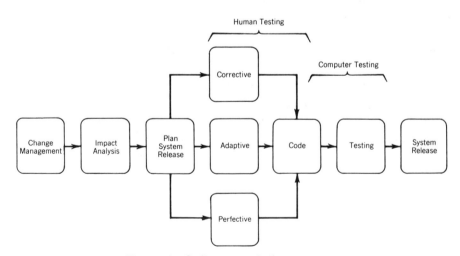

Figure 1   Software evolution process

product. Chapters 11 and 12 cover how to *implement* and *manage* a productive, high-quality maintenance environment.

I feel that a stationary maintenance environment is one headed for extinction. And that's what this book is all about: the evolution of software *and* the environment that supports it. They change constantly. Keeping up, or even getting ahead, is the software-maintenance challenge.

LOWELL JAY ARTHUR

De⸱⸱⸱er, Colorado
September 1987

Contents

CHAPTER

1

Software Evolution and Maintenance

In many ways software *maintenance* fails to describe the daily activities of the hordes of programmers and analysts who work on existing software. They constantly change software to meet the evolving needs of business, applications, and technology. In a typical environment these people actually spend less than 10% of their time fixing defects. They spend the majority of their time on enhancements—software evolution. Throughout this book you will see software maintenance and software evolution used interchangeably. *Software maintenance* means to preserve from failure or decline; *software evolution* means a continuous change from a lesser, simpler, or worse state to a higher or better state.

Because most organizations depend heavily on existing software systems, software maintenance is a critical function. Supporting these systems is the mission of the software maintainer.

To help you accomplish this mission, this chapter will:

• Explain the functions and flow of the software maintenance process.

1

- Define the three types of software maintenance: corrective, adaptive, and perfective.
- Identify the factors critical to successful, productive maintenance and evolution of software.

The major concern of software staffs today is how to maintain the existing portfolio of programs. Consider the following maintenance problems:

1. Most computer programs are difficult and expensive to maintain.

   One Air Force project cost $75 per line of code to build and $4000 per line to maintain.

   Software maintenance costs $300 billion each year worldwide, and demand is rapidly increasing (Martin 1983).

   Over the past 15 years the budget for maintenance has increased from approximately 50% of the resources expended on application software to 70–75%

   Each new development project adds to the maintenance burden. "Add little to little and you have a big pile!"

   End-user applications on micros, minis, and information centers will require maintenance.

   Demand for maintenance already exceeds the capabilities of most maintenance organizations. The user departments of businesses are programming many of their new applications. If maintenance is not managed and improved, demand will easily exceed available programming resources for both DP professionals and end users.

2. Software changes are poorly designed and implemented.

   Design documents are rarely examined and updated to reflect changes to the system.

   A carelessly planned system takes three times as long as estimated to complete; a carefully planned system takes only twice as long.

   Difficult-to-maintain systems are ultimately rewritten at great expense.

   The two years following the release of a new product are spent implementing enhancements to bring the system up to the user's *expectations*.

   Most major enhancements are so poorly understood and implemented that several additional releases are necessary to clean up the enhancement.

3. The repair and enhancement of software often injects new bugs that must later be repaired.

To resolve these problems and manage the growing software inventory, improvements are needed in the skills and productivity of maintainers, and in the quality and effectiveness of their work. This text focuses on helping you accomplish these goals.

To begin with, maintainers and managers should recognize that:

- Not all system maintainers are created equal, but they can be educated to equivalent skill levels.
- The difference between the best and worst performers is at least an order of magnitude.
- The reason for this disparity is a difference in the level of knowledge and skill, often referred to as *breakthrough* knowledge.
- The best performers can execute the key software maintenance activities more effectively than their counterparts.
- No single activity, or area of expertise, accounts for the differences.
- The key to maintenance productivity is to do most things a little better or faster (Peters 1985).
- A little more knowledge and skill multiplied over many activities produces striking differences in performance.

Providing maintainers with the lastest knowledge, skills, and techniques to achieve their mission by performing the key software maintenance activities a little better will reap significant productivity and quality improvements.

This text describes techniques for resolving many of the problems previously discussed. It describes the methods, tools, and techniques to improve your productivity and the quality of the software being maintained.

1. THE SOFTWARE LIFE CYCLE

The software life cycle covers the period from conception to retirement of a given software product. There are many definitions of the software life cycle. They differ primarily in the classifications of phases and activities. One traditional model is shown in Figure 1.1.

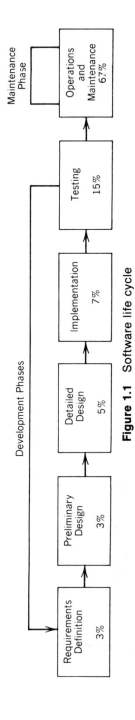

Figure 1.1 Software life cycle

As this diagram shows, for many large software systems, only one-fourth to one-third of all life-cycle costs are attributed to software development. The lions share of the effort and costs are spent in the operations and maintenance. (Note that the percentages indicate relative costs.)

2. SOFTWARE EVOLUTION ACTIVITIES

Software evolution consists of the activities required to keep a software system operational and responsive after it is accepted and placed into production. These activities include:

Correcting defects (maintenance)

Enhancing software functionality (evolution)

Improving the quality of existing software (maintenance)

In general, these activities keep the system in sync with an evolving, expanding user and operational environment. Functionally, software maintenance can be divided into these three categories:

Corrective   *Corrective maintenance* focuses on fixing defects. Defects refer to the system not performing as originally intended, or as specified in the requirements. There are a variety of situations that can be described as corrective maintenance. Some of them include:

Correcting a program that aborts.

Correcting a program that produces incorrect results.

Corrective maintenance is a *reactive* process. Defects generally need to be corrected either immediately or in the near future.

Adaptive   *Adaptive maintenance* includes all work related to changing how the software functions. Adaptive maintenance includes system changes, additions, insertions, deletions, modifications, extensions, and enhancements to meet the evolving needs of the user and the environment in which the system must operate. Adaptive maintenance is generally performed as a result of new or changing requirements. Some examples are:

Rearranging fields on an output report.

Changing a system to support new hardware configurations.

Adding a new function.

Deleting a function.

Converting a system from batch to on-line operation.

Making a program more efficient does *not* affect its functionality. As a result this type of change should be
considered as part of perfective maintenance.

Perfective   *Perfective maintenance* includes all efforts to improve the
quality of the software. These activities can include restructuring codes, creating and updating documentation, improving reliability or efficiency, or any other
qualities such as those discussed in Chapter 7 and 8.
Some specific examples are:

Improving efficiency, maintainability, or reliability
without changing functionality.

Restructuring code to make it more maintainable.

Tuning a system to reduce response time.

Although these three types of work are discussed separately in this
text, much of the work is performed concurrently. For example, enhancements and quality improvements are often worked and tested together.
Design of one program's changes will overlap the coding of another's. All
of these activities occur during the software maintenance life cycle.

3. MAINTENANCE AND DEVELOPMENT DIFFERENCES

Although many activities related to maintaining and developing software are similar, software maintenance has unique characteristics of its
own, including:

- *Constraints of an existing system.* Software maintenance is performed
  on an existing production system. Any changes must conform or be
  compatible with an existing architecture, design, and code constraints. Typically, the older the system, the more challenging and
  time consuming the maintenance effort becomes. Later chapters will
  discuss methods of preventing software extinction.

- *Shorter time frames.* Software development may span one or more
  years, whereas maintenance may span a few hours to cycles of one to

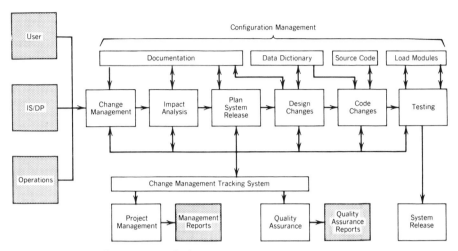

Figure 1.2 Software-maintenance data flow

six months. Chapters 2 and 4 will discuss the concept and implementation of software releases.

• *Available test data.* Software development creates all test data from scratch. Software maintenance can use this existing test data and perform regression tests. Thus the challenge is to create new data to adequately test the changes and their impact on the rest of the system. Chapter 9 will discuss testing strategies for software maintenance.

Software maintenance can, and should, be a structured process. It involves many different people and groups. Figure 1.2 illustrates the software maintenance process used in this text.

4. THE MAINTENANCE PROCESS

The maintenance process begins when a request for change is initiated by a user. (Note that a *user* is defined as anyone who uses or interacts with the system, including systems engineers, information systems personnel, data processing, operations, and marketing personnel.) It ends when the system passes testing, is accepted by the user, and is released for operation. In between, a variety of activities involving maintainers, quality assurance, configuration management, and test personnel must be planned for, coordinated, and implemented. These activities should be coordinated by use of change management.

4.1.　Change Management

The basic objective of change management is to uniquely identify, describe, and track the status of each requested change.

A *change request* is a vehicle for recording information about a system defect, requested enhancement, or quality improvement.

The major change management activities are:

1. Enter change requests. Maintainers receive a request for some type of change (i.e., defect, enhancement, and quality improvement), analyze the change, and generate a change request.

   In this text a system is defined as a group of programs (business environment) or configuration items (DOD environment).

   A program/configuration item is an executable piece of software made up of many modules or units.

   A module is equivalent to a unit. It consists of object or source language code that, under the precepts of structured programming, implements a single function.

2. Track change requests and provide regular or exception reports on the status of change requests.

3. Provide an audit trail of changes.

4. Provide input to project management and quality assurance systems.

Change management is discussed more fully in Chapter 2. Once a change is initiated, an analyst has to evaluate its impact on the existing system and estimate the resources needed to complete the change.

4.2.　Impact Analysis

The overall objective of impact analysis is to determine the scope of the requested change as a basis for planning and implementing it.

The major impact analysis tasks are:

1. Evaluate change requests for potential impacts on existing systems, other systems, documentation, hardware, data structures, and humans (users, maintainers, and operators).

2. Develop a preliminary resource estimate.

3. Document the scope of the requested change and update the change request.

Impact analysis is covered in depth in Chapter 3. Once these changes have been analyzed, they can be grouped together as a scheduled maintenance release. This requires planning.

4.3. System Release Planning

The principle objective of system release planning is to determine the contents and timing of system releases.

The major system release planning tasks are:

1. Rank and select change requests for the next release.
2. Batch the changes, by work product, and schedule the work.
3. Prepare a system release planning document (Version Description Document for the DOD), and place it under control of the configuration management system.
4. Update approved change requests.

When system release planning occurs varies depending on whether you work in a contractual or noncontractual environment. When maintenance is done under contract, the contents and timing of a system release are negotiated and agreed to before any major work is begun, unless the contract is a *level-of-effort* contract.

Naturally, to agree on a contract, some level of analysis must be done to determine the scope of the changes and the resources required. When maintenance is done without a contract (i.e., in-house), a release is planned after the change requests have been analyzed and the scope of work is clearly understood.

System release planning is discussed in greater detail in Chapter 4. Once a release is planned, maintainers can design the change.

4.4. Design Changes

The major objective of the design phase is to develop a revised *logical* and *physical* design for the approved changes. Logical design relates to the system level, and physical design relates to the program level.

The major design activities are:

1. Analyze the approved change and review the structure of the target system, program, or module.
2. Revise or develop the logical and physical designs.

3. Design hardware and data transmission changes, if necessary.
4. Update the system and program design documents, as well as the data dictionary, to reflect any changes.
5. Restore or place all documents under control of the configuration management system.
6. Update the change request to reflect the documents revised during design.

System and program design is covered for each of the three types of maintenance: in Chapter 5, corrective maintenance; in Chapter 6, adaptive maintenance; and in Chapter 7, perfective maintenance. Once the designs have been changed, maintainers can proceed to coding the change.

4.5. Coding

The objective of coding is to change the software to reflect the approved changes represented in the system (logical) program (physical) designs.
The major coding activities are:

1. Implement and review all changes to code.
2. Restore or place the source code under control of the configuration management system.
3. Update the change request to reflect the modules or units changed.

Coding changes are discussed further in Chapter 8. The next step in the maintenance process puts the revised designs and code to test.

4.6. Testing

The primary objective of testing is to ensure compliance with the original requirements and the approved changes. I advocate an incremental testing strategy—one that weeds out bugs along the way, not when most of the work is done.
The major testing activities are:

1. Human testing:
    Requirements, design, and code *walk-throughs* or *inspections*.
2. Computer testing:
    Unit test all code changes by module or unit.

Integration test the interfaces between each module of the program and the program as a whole.

System test the interfaces between programs to ensure that the system meets all of the original requirements plus the added changes.

Acceptance testing, where the user approves the revised system.

Chapter 9 discusses testing in more detail. Once a system has been thoroughly tested and accepted, it can be released for use.

4.7. System Release

The objective of system release is to deliver the system and updated documentation to users for installation and operation.

The major activity associated with releasing a system is to package the release and send it to the user. System release packaging organizes all of the products of the maintenance project—user manuals, software, data definitions, and job control language—for delivery to the client or user. System delivery methods vary from mail to floppy disks to telecommunications.

Chapter 10 discusses system release and configuration management in more detail.

5. SOFTWARE EVOLUTION

Software evolution and maintenance are presented in this text as linear or sequential processes. There are, however, a number of activities that require overlaps and interative loops. Some examples include recycling emergency repairs through the scheduled release process, returning change requests for clarification, additional analysis and estimation after an impact analysis, and additional design and coding changes after testing discovers bugs. Usually these processes occur synchronously throughout the maintenance staff (e.g., a systems analyst works on program design *B* while programmers revise the code in program *A*).

This book describes what must be done to maximize productivity and quality. Due to your own local resource constraints, this may not be possible or desirable. The process must be tailored to each specific environment. For example, simple, noncritical systems and changes may loosely follow the process, whereas complex, critical systems and changes will need more stringent controls.

Critical systems include DOD mission critical software, accounts receivable and payable, inventory control, payroll, billing, and manufacturing control. Noncritical systems handle functions that can be delayed, such as capacity planning, status reporting, annual reporting, and marketing.

Although they may be handled loosely in some less crucial environments, the following factors are critical to effectively conducting software evolution and maintenance:

- Develop and adhere to a well-defined and structured software maintenance methodology. Know when and how to tailor it to fit your environment.
- Use structured design and coding techniques.
- Control changes and software products with change and configuration management systems.
- Conduct an impact analysis of all requested changes before agreeing to do them.
- Establish scheduled releases and batch change requests to maximize productivity and quality.
- Measure and gather quality assurance data, and use it to refine and improve software development and maintenance practices.
- Use incremental testing to improve the quality of delivered software.
- Introduce and use modern, automated tools to improve quality and productivity.
- Obtain management's support for software evolution.

6. SUMMARY

Software maintenance consists of the activities required to keep a software system operational and responsive after it is accepted and placed into production.

The key differences between maintenance and development are:

- Constraints of an existing system
- Shorter time frames
- Available test data

Software evolution consists of three key activities:

- Corrective maintenance—fixing defects
- Adaptive maintenance—enhancing existing systems
- Perfective maintenance—improving software quality

This text uses a seven-process approach to represent the software maintenance process. Those processes are:

- Managing change
- Analyzing impacts
- Planning system releases
- Designing changes
- Coding changes
- Testing changes
- Releasing the system

DISCUSSION QUESTIONS

1. What are some of the characteristics of productive software maintenance?

2. What are some characteristics of maintaining software as opposed to developing new systems?

3. Based on your experience, what are some other characteristics of maintaining software?

4. What are some of the typical problems, or challenges that you face as a software-maintenance professional?

5. What are some of the benefits of using a structured approach to software maintenance?

6. Which of the critical success factors do you think is the most important, and why?

7. Which are the most difficult to do consistently well, and why?

2

Change Management

Your supervisor receives a call about the status of a user's change request. The supervisor asks you about it, but you've passed it to Mary, the analyst, who's passed it to two programmers, and all five of you powwow to figure out its status. Meanwhile you've forgotten what you were working on when you were interrupted.

A client calls with a problem that sounds like something you fixed several months ago. It seems, however, that whoever took the request didn't document it or it slipped into a crack in the papermill. You can't even remember where you fixed the problem, so you spend a half a day reworking the change only to discover that it *has* already been fixed and the user ran the wrong version of the program.

Your manager comes in and requests a status report of your activities for the last three months. You can't remember what you've done in the last three days, let alone three months. Wouldn't it be nice to have a system that tracks all of your work for you?

After releasing a system, the user complains that the new change doesn't work the way it should. You say, "It works the way you told me over the phone." The user responds, "I didn't tell you that." And you can't find the piece of paper you wrote the description on. Your supervisor admonishes you for not doing a good job and you have to change the system again.

The preceding examples illustrate some of the problems in a software maintenance environment where an inadequate or no change management system was used. This chapter will help you:

- Understand the purpose of a change management system.
- Recognize the benefits of managing change.
- Understand the purpose and contents of a change request.

1. CHANGE MANAGEMENT

Change management is a methodology for controlling change to evolving systems. Although they are called many things, problem reports and enhancement requests are the two components of most change management systems.

- Problem reports describe defects and system actions that are out of line with the system's requirements. Consider the example of an airline reservation system that incorrectly assigns seats.
- Enhancement requests describe a change in system requirements, functionality, or quality—for example, enabling travel agencies to issue boarding passes with tickets.

Because both of these items represent a request to *change* an existing system, they will be referred to as a single entity, a *change request,* throughout this text. Closer examination will show that they both require the same information and can be represented by a single document.

Figure 2.1 shows how changes flow through a software maintenance project.

- The data flow diagram shows the change management function and how it fits into the overall software maintenance process.
- The diagram in upper left-hand corner shows that change management is the first step in the overall software maintenance process.
- The exploded change management diagram shows a requested change as input.

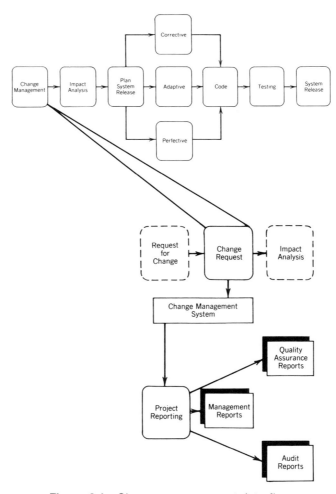

Figure 2.1 Change management data flow

These problem reports or enhancement requests are documented as a change request.

- Change requests are placed under control of the change management system.

  Change management systems control change by either a manual method or automated system.

- Data from the change management system feeds into the project reporting system.

This system produces a variety of project management reports, quality assurance reports, and audit trails.

- Having initiated a change request, it is passed to an analyst for evaluation of its impact.
- Later, when the change request has been approved, it can be folded into a scheduled system release.
- Then plans for implementing the change are developed.
- Maintainers then design, code, and test the software or documentation in preparation for release.
- The change request is updated, via the change management system, at every step along the way.

Change requests document all essential information about requested and approved changes to a system. Change requests can be manual (i.e., typed or handwritten) or electronic (i.e., input through a terminal to a data base). Regardless of the medium, change requests should be updated, just like other software and documentation products, throughout the maintenance process.

The objectives of change management are to:

- Provide a common method of communication among maintainers, management, and users.
- Uniquely identify and track the status of each change request. This feature simplifies progress reporting and provides better control over changes.
- Maintain an information base about all changes to the system. This information can be used for status reporting, project management, auditing, and quality assurance.

Another important part of change control is to manage the different versions of documentation and software delivered to users. *Configuration management* handles the control of all products/configuration items and changes to those items. (Products/configuration items include documents, software, source code, hardware, tapes, disks, and computer listings.)

Many people consider configuration management to be a roadblock, a part of the job they simply tolerate. In reality configuration management plays a major role in ensuring the quality of the delivered system and the productivity of the system maintainers. Configuration management should not be taken lightly. It ensures that approved products are not contaminated by uncontrolled or unapproved changes.

The objectives of configuration management are to:

* Uniquely identify every version of every product/configuration item.
* Retain historical versions of software and documentation.
* Provide an audit trail of all changes.

Change and configuration management are methods for controlling all changes to software, hardware, and documentation. When changes are controlled via these two methodologies, maintainers can work more productively and communicate more effectively.

2. CHANGE REQUESTS

As previously stated, a change request is the basic tool of a change management system. Because a change request contains essential information about changes to the software, it can serve a wide variety of needs, not just those of the maintainer. If one thinks about how a change request could be used, a key group of change management functions should emerge. Consider these examples:

* Document what to do, how well, and by when.

    The maintenance process begins when a change request is initiated. Everyone who uses or interacts with the system, including maintainers, users, and managers, can initiate a change request. Whoever enters the change request (typically a user) must describe the requested change in sufficient detail to enable another person to understand accurately the problem or requested change, assess its impacts, and approve or reject the request.

    By documenting new software requirements or requirements that are not being met, the change request becomes the *contract* between the person requesting the change and the maintainers who work the change.

    Once a change request is generated, it is the maintainers responsibility to keep it current.

* Communicate a variety of information about changes among maintainers, managers, and clients.

    The change request communicates the client's needs to the maintainers. It communicates the maintenance work that has been done from system architect to designer to programmer to tester. It communicates the status of the change from maintainer to manager or user.

- Track changes to help manage the system release.

  By documenting who is responsible for a change and information about the schedule, budget, and status of the change, managers and maintainers can monitor and control the work effort to ensure delivery of the system release on schedule and within budget.

- Provide information about changes and the origin of productivity and quality problems in software maintenance. Analysis of the types and frequency of defects can serve to improve both the development and maintenance processes.

- By documenting what was changed, why, and by whom, the information can be used by quality assurance personnel and system maintainers to streamline the maintenance process and reduce costs.

As shown in Figure 2.2, a variety of people use the change management system as the central point for documenting, communicating, tracking, maintaining, and reporting changes. The users of a change management system include:

- *Maintainers,* who use the system to communicate about system changes and to report project status.
- *Managers,* who use the system to monitor and report project status.
- *Users,* who initiate change requests and receive reports on status, schedules, and other information as needed.
- *Auditors,* who use the system to trace changes, evaluate adherence to policies, generate audit reports, and for on-line inquiry.
- *Quality assurance personnel,* who use the data captured by the system to analyze quality soft spots and to generate recommendations for change.

3. CHANGE REQUEST CONTENTS

To accommodate its variety of uses without becoming unwieldy, a change request should document *essential information* about changes to soft-

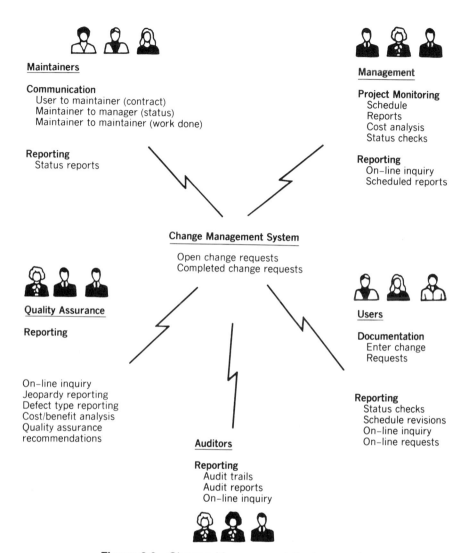

Figure 2.2 Change Management Environment

ware, hardware, and documentation. The definition of "essential information" is unique to every organization. However, a minimum set of information is required to meet the needs of the personnel shown in Figure 2.2.

The minimum contents of a change request are listed next. Each item is described in more detail on subsequent pages.

CHANGE REQUEST CONTENTS

Identification number	Problem origin
Originator	Resolution
Date originated	Impacts
Date required	Maintenance phase
Maintenance type	Phase start date
Severity of change	Approval
System	Personnel assigned
Program	Estimated resources
Change description	Actual resources
Anticipated benefits	

A description of each item contained on the change request follows:

Unique number	This identification number allows the change request to be traced throughout the maintenance process. A suggested format would have the year, month, and a unique number: YYMMNNN.
Originator	(of the change request) This information is needed for tracking purposes and for clarification of the requested change.
Date originated	How long has it been since the originator requested this change?
Date required	Date when the revised system must be installed to meet business commitments.
Maintenance type	Classify the work as *corrective, adaptive,* or *perfective* maintenance. The process for each type of work is different. This information tells the maintainer something about the nature of the work, and it indicates to management how maintenance time is spent. This information can be used to analyze program quality (see Chapter 7).
Change severity	This rating, applied to change requests, indicates a different time frame for completion. This program uses a four-point rating scale that represents the severity of requested changes. Severity codes are:

Severity 1. System is down, or system outputs are causing catastrophic problems.

For example, federal withholding tax is calculated incorrectly shorting the government anywhere from $20 to $500 per paycheck. Although this may not be considered catastrophic by employees, it is an example of a severity 1 change request.

However, a report program that aborts, but is not needed for two weeks, is *not* an example of a severity 1 change request. It should be considered a severity 2.

Severity 2. System is operational and can be manually overridden or ignored until a specific date. Severity 2 change requests may upgrade to severity 1's if the problem is not fixed by the date required.

An example of a severity 2 change request is a program that truncates the CEO's paycheck from $12,000 to $2,000. Because a check can be issued manually to override the problem until the next pay period, it may not be considered a severity 1 change.

However, a payroll report program that incorrectly prints everyone's payroll number (*not* social security number) is *not* an example of a severity 2 change. Because it can be fixed in the next scheduled release, it would be classified as a severity 3 change.

Severity 3. Includes all repairs and enhancements that can be deferred until the next scheduled system release. For example, adding a new report to the system, or correcting a subtotal on a noncritical report.

Moving a field around on a report is *not* an example of a severity 3 change request because the data is already available on the report page. This request should be classified as a severity 4 and handled as time permits.

Severity 4. Includes all minor repairs or enhancements. They should be worked into the next scheduled system release as resources allow.

An example of a severity 4 change is enhancing a program to print totals of records read and written when the program finishes. This feature may be nice for operations, but it is of limited value to the user.

Whether your organization uses a similar classification scheme or defines these classifications differently is *not* particularly important. What is important is that some classification is used to highlight the magnitude, criticality, or complexity of change requests. Now let's continue with the key elements of a change request.

System
: Identify the system where the change is needed or the problem occurred.

Program
: Identify the program where the change is needed (if known), or where the problem occurred. Both the system and program affected are used as starting points for the three types of maintenance.

Change description
: This should include a functional or technical description of the requested change. If well documented, the information contained in the description enables maintainers to react quickly to problems, analyze enhancements properly, evaluate impacts, and estimate resources.

The description of the requested change should cover the items that follow. Each item is a clue about user needs. Note that not all of the items are necessary or relevant for all changes. Nor is this list all inclusive. The most important thing to remember is that the change description should be complete and clear. It should include many of the following:

Purpose of change

Hardware, operating system, or teleprocessing environment in which the change will run (i.e., IBM 30XX/VM)

Domain of valid input values and range of valid output values

Functions required and algorithms used to implement the change

Input and output formats

Operating instructions

Options for implementing the change

Run time (i.e., efficiency)

Accuracy required

Quality requirements

Benefits	Tangible or intangible benefits of doing the change. This is used to aid the technical review board in ranking and approving all requested changes.
Problem origin	Too often, problem descriptions only identify where a problem was fixed. Because a defect in one program may be traced to incorrect specifications for a program in a different system, it is important to know where the problem originated. This information is key to improving quality and reducing maintenance costs.
Resolution	Documenting what was changed, how, and why are essential ingredients in audit trails and quality analysis.
Impacts	Knowing which products are affected by a change and the ripple effect of a proposed change is necessary to estimate accurately the scope of work and the resources required.
Phase	Design, code, test, released, installed, and so forth, for tracking purposes.
Phase start date	Date phase begins. This information is used for progress reporting and project management.
Approvals	Approval should be obtained at a variety of checkpoints. At a minimum, approval should be obtained to start the work and following testing to approve the delivered product. Each milestone in the maintenance process can also be approved—impact analysis, design, code, test, and release.
Personnel assigned	Name of person(s) assigned to do the work.
Estimated resources	The original and revised cost and schedule estimates. This information can also be used as a reference for similar work on other projects, or future releases.
Actual resources	This information allows verification of the original estimates and estimating process.

A change request that contains less information than the minimum set described carries varying degrees of risk. Some of the key risks are:

- Changes may be lost or misunderstood.
- Work may be poorly focused, reducing productivity.
- Insufficient information may remain about how the change was made. Adequate information can aid future maintainers.
- Quality assurance information may be unavailable, making it difficult to analyze the maintenance process and identify areas for improvement. Without such information it is difficult to reconstruct why some changes are worked smoothly and others are a problem.
- No audit trail may exist of what was changed and why. This is especially sensitive in financial systems.

Three sample change requests are contained on the following pages. The samples show the minimum amount of information needed to track and document changes. Each sample reflects one of the three types of maintenance (corrective, adaptive, perfective).

Take a few minutes to review each one. Pay particular attention to contents and level of detail. Some key points to note about the change requests are:

1. Each change request has a different identification number for tracking purposes. It consists of the year, month, and a unique number for that month.
2. Each change request shows a different originator. The second two change requests use possible titles for the originator. In reality these should be actual names of people. Names enable a maintainer to contact the originator when questions arise. Names also enable auditors to trace the source of a change.
3. The type of maintenance is different for each of the three changes—corrective, adaptive, and perfective. This affects the process used to accomplish the change.
4. Change 8603-002 is a severity 1, which implies an emergency repair as reflected in the phase of maintenance. The other two are both severity 3 changes, meaning that they should be worked in the next scheduled release.
5. The program affected is most useful for corrective and perfective maintenance work. It provides a place to start looking for the defect, or where to improve the code.

CHANGE REQUEST

Identification number: 8603-002
Originator: L. J. Green NASA
Date originated: 03/04/86
Date required: 03/04/86
Type: Corrective
Severity code: 1
System: Titan Launch
Program: Ascent
Change description: Restore satellite to its specified oribit. The incorrect ascent trajectory is putting satellite into earth's lower orbit.
Anticipated benefits: Satellite orbit will decay in two years, costing $80 million to replace the vehicle. Unable to continue launch program without correction.
Problem origin:
  System: Titan
  Program: Ascent
  Module: Initialization
  Type of error: Invalid initial loads
Resolution: Correct initialization loads to correct ascent profile.

Impacts:
  Systems: Titan
  Programs: Ascent
  Modules: Initialization
  Documentation: Initialization specification
Phase: Emergency maintenance
  Phase start date: 03/05/86
  Approval: Tom Prieve
  Personnel assigned: Jay Arthur
  Estimated resources: 2 person days
  Actual resources: 1.5 person days

CHANGE REQUEST

Identification number:	8603-006
Originator:	Project manager
Date originated:	03/19/86
Date required:	05/01/86
Type:	Adaptive
Severity code:	3
System:	Terrain Following Radar
Program:	Map mode
Change description:	Using the expanded capabilities of the B-1 phased array radar antenna, add a larger (18.5 kilometer square) map of the terrain to the synthetic-aperature mode of the radar.
Benefits:	Wider field of view for pilots at low levels in the B-1 and stealth bombers.
Resolution:	
Impacts:	
Systems:	
Programs:	
Modules:	
Documentation:	
Hardware:	
Telecommunications:	
Phase:	Requirements definition
Phase start date:	04/01/86
Approval:	Col. Greene.
Personnel assigned:	Systems analyst
Estimated resources:	_____ person days
Actual resources:	_____ person days

CHANGE REQUEST

Identification number:	8602-003
Originator:	Senior technician
Date originated:	02/01/86
Date required:	05/01/86
Type:	Perfective
Severity code:	3
System:	Payroll System
Program:	PE15
Change description:	Revise the PE15 Data Base Wage and Tax Segment to allow access and update to the PE15 Data Base by the tax department.
Anticipated benefits:	Reduce maintenance of the Wage and Tax Segment of the PE15 Data Base, by allowing tax department control of data.
	Prevent unauthorized access to the
	Current Wage Field
	Adjusted Wage Field
	Gross Wages Field
Resolution:	Change the Physical Data Base Design of the PE15 Data Base from Segment Level Sensitivity to Field Level Sensitivity.
	Change all Payroll Programs accessing the Wage and Tax Segment to access by field.
	Change all intersystem and intrasystem files to contain only the Wage and Tax Segment fields required by the interfacing programs and systems.
	Revise documentation and operational procedures for the Wage and Tax Segment.
Impacts:	
Systems:	Payroll
Programs:	PE15
Modules:	PE1501, PE1503, PE1504, PE1516
Documentation:	Payroll system design, PE15 program design, Wage and Tax Segment requirements, and operational procedures for PE15.
Hardware:	None
Telecommunications:	None
Phase:	Preliminary design
Phase start date:	02/15/86
Approval:	Manager
Personnel assigned:	Senior technician
	Data adminsitration
Estimated resources:	65 person days
Actual resources:	_____ person days

PERSONNEL RESPONSIBLE FOR ENTERING
AND UPDATING CHANGE REQUEST INFORMATION

Item	MGT	SM	JM	PRG	User
Id number		*System Generated*			
Originator	E	E	E	E	E
Date originated	E	E	E	E	E
Date required	E,U	E,U	E,U	E	E
Type	E,U	E,U	E	E	E
Severity code	E,U	E,U	E	E	E
System	E	E,U	E,U	E,U	E
Program	E	E,U	E,U	E,U	E
Change description	E,U	E,U	E,U	E,U	E,U
Benefits	E,U	E,U	E,U	E,U	E,U
Problem origin	E,U	E,U	E,U	E,U	E,U
Resolution		E,U	E,U	E,U	
Impacts		E,U	E,U		
Phase	U	E,U	U	U	U
Phase start date	E,U	U			
Approval	E,U				U
Personnel assigned		E	E		
Estimated resources		E,U	E,U		
Actual resources	E,U	E,U			

Legend
  E = Enter
  U = Update

Figure 2.3 Change management system access

As previously mentioned, the people responsible for entering and updating information on the change request varies depending on the maintenance environment. A matrix indicating who might enter and update
each item of the change request is shown in Figure 2.3. Notice that
functional titles are listed across the top of the matrix:

MGT (management)

SM (senior maintainer)

JM (junior maintainer)

PRG (programmer)

User

The contents of the change request are listed down the first column under ITEM. The legend is at the bottom of the page: "E" means enter; "U" means update. As you review the diagram, jot down who in your organization would enter and update the change request information.

4. EVALUATING CHANGE REQUESTS

Since change requests are used to document and communicate information to a wide variety of people, it is important to include enough information to meet the needs of these people. At a minimum a change request should identify:

- What is to be changed?
- Why will it be changed?
- How will it be changed?
- When will it be changed?
- What is the budget?
- Where will it be changed?
- Who will make the change?
- Is the description clear and concise? Are all clues and leads adequately described to allow impact analysis to begin?
- If not, is the originator available for clarification?
- What information is extraneous to the request?

Throughout the maintenance process, you will have to use the change request as a source of information. To evaluate a change request, you should look for information that answers the preceding questions.

Evaluating changes requests is easy; getting all of the right information usually isn't.

5. IMPLEMENTATION CONSIDERATIONS

If you have a change management system, ask yourself if it fulfills all of the uses described on the preceding pages. If you do not have a change management system, you may find the following discussion of benefit.

A change management system may be manual, automated, or some combination of the two. The following paragraphs describe considerations for implementing manual and automated change management systems.

5.1. Manual Systems

To implement a manual change management system:

- Develop a paper form containing the minimum information needed for communication among the users, maintainers, and management.
- Store the change requests in a central library or file for ready examination by maintainers, management, and users. Use copies of the central form for all maintenance processes.
- Update the form as each phase of the maintenance process completes.

Manual systems suffer from a number of potentially serious problems:

- Manually prepared forms are rarely updated.
- Manual forms are easily lost.
- The change request data used may be of questionable reliability.
- Manual forms require manual compilation and reporting which:
    Is not prompt enough to manage projects adequately
    Prone to error
    Not productive

5.2. Automated Systems

An automated change management system contains the same information as a manual system but allows for timely and productive inquiry to facilitate project management, status reporting, auditing, and quality assurance. An automated system is also more reliable than written forms, both in content and in security. Maintainers like to use terminals, not forms, to enter data. Also the data is current, backed up, and secure within the system. It is not floating on someone's desk.

To implement an automated change management system:

- Use an existing, canned package, or develop a system from scratch using a data base management system to maximize its utility and flexibility.

- In selecting or developing a change management system, think about the following:

    The system should be flexible because, like any system, once users get their hands on the product, enhancements will be needed. Typical changes include new fields and reports.

    The system should allow flexible reporting levels. It should make allowances for:

    detailed information about the change,

    project management information,

    progress reports,

    summaries of change information,

    inquiry capability, and

    regular feedback to maintainers.

As shown in Figure 2.4, a change management system should be linked with as many existing systems as possible. There are various features and benefits of such configurations to consider:

- When linked to an electronic mail system, the combination can be used to deliver memos and reports on project developments and status to project personnel. It can also be used to notify personnel of their assignment to a change request.

- When linked to a configuration management system, the two systems can be used to control and track changes and the products being changed.

    Together, they provide a complete audit trail from change request to the final product.

    Together, they improve change control because personnel are unable to modify system documents, code, or program without a valid, approved change request.

- When linked to word processing, it can speed up documentation development and revisions. It can facilitate editing any status or project management report into other documents (for management or clients).

- When linked to a project management system, the CM system assists management in tracking budgets and schedules and in assessing project progress.

- When linked to a quality assurance system to identify quality data, such as date of defect, type of defect, defect resolution, and problem

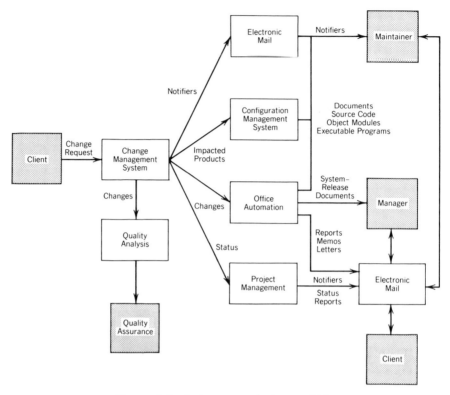

Figure 2.4   Software evolution tool kit

description, the resulting data enables recurring maintenance problems to be detected and prevented. For example, a recurring problem
might involve using uninitialized fields. This may suggest a quality
assurance mandate to initialize all fields.

The limitations of an automated change management system are essentially the same as a manual system. The information in the system is
only as good as the data the maintainers enter into it. An automated
system with poor data is a poor system. Without good data, quality analysis will fail to improve the maintenance process, reduce costs, and improve the quality of the system.

A change management system can be either manual or automated.
Regardless of method, it is critical that the change management system
be implemented and used.

6. SUMMARY

Change management is an ongoing activity throughout the software evolution process. The initiation of a change request is the first phase of the process. The key is to enter and update change requests as changes progress through the software evolution life cycle.

The main points of this chapter are that:

- Change management is a method for controlling all requests for changes.
- Configuration management is a method for controlling all product/ configuration items and changes to those items.
- When changes are controlled, maintainers are able to work productively and communicate effectively.

Contrary to popular opinion, a change management system does *not* hinder productivity. It improves it. Some other benefits of using a change management system are that:

- Changes are documented in terms of what to do, how well, and by when.
- Changes can be tracked and monitored to ensure delivery of the system release on time and within budget.
- Various quality assurance and productivity data can be maintained and reported to improve the maintenance process.
- Changes are communicated to all concerned in a timely manner.

  Maintainers use the system to communicate changes and to report project status. They can also use the system to document their work efforts.

  Managers use the system to monitor and report project status.

  Users initiate change requests and receive reports on status, schedules, and other information as needed.

  Auditors use the system to trace changes, evaluate adherence to policies, generate audit reports, and for on-line inquiry.

  Quality assurance personnel use the data captured by the system to analyze quality soft spots and to generate recommendations for change.

The basic contents of a change request should include a description of:

Identification number	Problem origin
Originator	Resolution
Date originated	Impacts
Date required	Maintenance phase
Maintenance type	Phase start date
Severity of change	Approval
System	Personnel assigned
Program	Estimated resources
Change description	Actual resources
Anticipated benefits	

When evaluating a change request, determine:

• What will be changed.
• Why it will be changed.
• How it will be changed.
• When it will be changed.
• What the budget is.
• Where it will be changed.
• Who will make the change.
• If the description is clear and concise, are all clues and leads adequately described to allow impact analysis to begin?
• If not, is the originator available for clarification?
• What information is extraneous to the request.

To meet the software evolution challenge, change management addresses the following critical success factors:

• Controlling software products and capturing data about the software maintenance process through the change management and configuration management systems.
• Using modern, automated tools to improve quality and productivity.

This chapter has touched on the features and benefits of a change management system, the minimum contents of a change request, and some of the things to think about when evaluating one.

The next chapter describes how to determine the impact of the proposed change on the existing system as well as other systems, programs, modules, or documentation.

DISCUSSION QUESTIONS

1. What are some of the problems associated with an inadequate change management system?

2. How do these problems affect your job?

3. What steps can you take to demonstrate the value of change management?

4. How would each of the following groups use the information contained in the change request?
   a. Maintainers?
   b. Management?
   c. Users?
   d. Quality assurance personnel?
   e. Auditors?

5. What are some of the items you would think about when reviewing a change request?

3

Impact Analysis

A change that appears simple can be much larger than anyone would expect. Without a proper impact analysis, resource estimates are grossly understated, and schedules are jeopardized.

Have you ever begun work on a change only to discover that it impacted an entire data base, most of the system documentation, or a large portion of the programs in the system?

Have you ever implemented a change only to have a downstream program or system abort because of your change?

Have you ever had a hard time estimating the resources needed to work a change because of:

- Poor documentation?
- Lack of a local guru who knows the system inside and out?
- Poor description of the requested change?

Have you ever had a user request a seemingly minor change, and refuse to understand its implications?

Impact analysis can help communicate the complexity of even a seemingly minor change. It also improves the quality of estimates because all impacted products—software, hardware, and documentation—are identified for revision.

Chapter 2 showed you how a change request can be documented and updated throughout the software maintenance process. With it and various system documents, you have all of the information needed to learn about the system and determine the impact of a change.

Impact analysis identifies all systems and system products affected by a change request and develops an estimate of the resources needed to accomplish the change. This chapter will help you:

- Understand the process for conducting an impact analysis
- Select tools for conducting an impact analysis
- Evaluate quality of an impact analysis and the process used to complete the analysis

The objectives of impact analysis are to:

1. Determine the scope of the change as a basis for planning and implementing work.
2. Develop accurate estimates of resources needed to accomplish the work.
3. Analyze cost/benefits of the requested change.
4. Communicate to others the complexity of a given change.

As shown in Figure 3.1, impact analysis is conducted after a change request has been entered in the change management system and before the system release is planned.

As you view the diagram, notice that impact analysis begins by reviewing the change request. Once a maintainer understands the problem or enhancement, the maintainer can begin to determine the impact of the change on existing systems, other systems, data structures, documentation, hardware, telecommunications, and users. The analyst uses information from the system requirements document, system and program design documents, and data dictionary to complete the impact analysis.

- A *system requirements document* specifies the system's functions and performance, from the user's perspective.
- *System and program design documents* specify the system's architec-

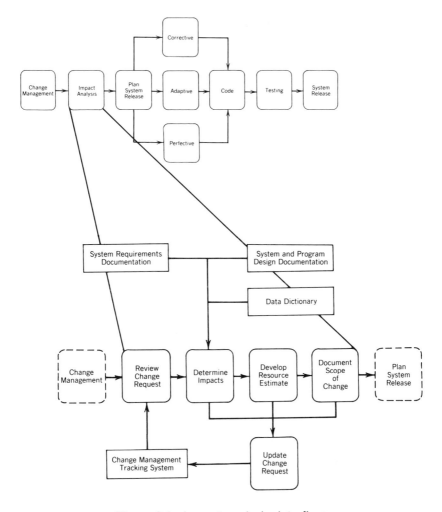

Figure 3.1 Impact analysis data flow

ture, data flow, functions performed, and the structure and functions of each program.

- The *data dictionary* is a mechanized data base of all data items, groups, and structures used by the system.

Once the maintainer determines the impact and ripple effect of a change, preliminary resource estimates are developed. These estimates are approximations of the work required to accomplish the changes to all affected parts of the system—code, documentation, hardware, and so forth. Estimates can be expressed in terms of days, weeks, hours, or any other unit of measurement most meaningful to the organization.

Finally, the maintainer updates the change request to include the scope of the change—a description of all items affected by the change. These items include:

- Programs/configuration items and modules/units
- Other systems (including those downstream from the change)
- Data bases or files
- Data items
- Documentation
- Hardware
- Human factors

This information is essential to the next phase of the maintenance life cycle—system release planning, the maintenance staff that will work the change, and the auditors and quality assurance personnel who will examine the data.

1. IMPACT ANALYSIS

This section describes a top-down approach for conducting an impact analysis. It presents the documents used to conduct an impact analysis and shows their relationships.

Maintainers should use a top-down approach to evaluate the scope and complexity of a change. A top-down approach begins with the highest, or broadest picture of the system. The analysis continues down through the program and module levels. It ends with the code.

Using a top-down approach ensures that all impacts are identified; the maintainer can see the "big" picture first and successively refine the impacts.

For example, to analyze the impact of a change, a maintainer would do the following:

1. Review change request.
2. Translate the change description into systems terminology.
3. Obtain user sign-off on the translated specifications.

4. Trace impacts to other systems, documents, hardware, and human factors by reviewing:

> System requirements
>
> System design documents
>
> Program design documents
>
> Module design documents
>
> Data dictionary

5. Develop resource estimates

6. Update the change request to show the scope of the change and the resources required.

The documents used to conduct an impact analysis and their relationships are shown in Figure 3.2. As you review the diagram, pay particular attention to the documents associated with each level of analysis. Also notice that the analysis performed at lower levels is a refinement of earlier work.

In reviewing any document, you should look for *clues* about the nature of changes to:

- Inputs
- Outputs
- Processing
- Interfaces
- Data flows
- Data stores
- Human factors
- Hardware
- Other systems
- Other documents

Analyzing the documents shown in Figure 3.2 is critical to a solid impact analysis. Without this analysis the change may insert defects that are not immediately apparent. The injection of new or hidden defects is one reason for the current volume of corrective maintenance work.

The most common problems with analyzing system documents are that they:

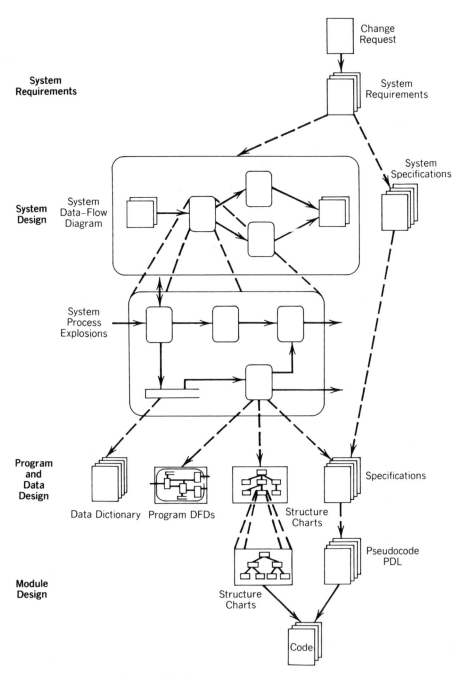

System Requirements

Change Request

System Requirements

System Specifications

System Design

System Data-Flow Diagram

System Process Explosions

Program and Data Design

Data Dictionary   Program DFDs

Structure Charts

Specifications

Module Design

Structure Charts

Pseudocode PDL

Code

Figure 3.2   Design document evolution

44

- Don't exist and must be created (this can be done manually or with automated documentation generators).

- Are out of date or incorrect, which is often worse because it can lead to incorrect design decisions. Again, in this situation the documents should be updated or generated.

As previously stated, impact analysis is a systematic method used to determine the impact of a change on systems, other systems, documentation, hardware, telecommunications, and people. Maintainers should use a top-down approach to conduct an impact analysis. Using a top-down approach ensures that all impacts are identified. The following example shows how to perform an impact analysis.

2. IMPACT ANALYSIS EXAMPLE

The following walks through a top-down impact analysis. The example is an enhancement to develop an on-line function that supports customer inquiries.

The activities described in this reading are:

- Review change request
- Translate change description into systems terminology
- User review
- Identify hardware impacts
- Identify system impacts
- Identify data impacts
- Identify program impacts
- Identify module impacts
- Identify document impacts
- Identify human impacts

2.1. Review Change Request

Before an impact analysis can be conducted, a preliminary review of the change request and other system documents is necessary. This review gets the maintainer "up-to-speed" on the requested changes and the system. It also verifies the accuracy and completeness of information provided on the change request.

When looking at the change request, a maintainer should determine if the description of the requested change is clear, concise, and current. If it isn't, contact the originator for clarification. (See Chapter 2 for the elements of a clear change description.) For this example no clarification is needed.

Figure 3.3 is an sample change request for the ACE Co. Review the change request to familiarize yourself with the change. Pay particular attention to the change description section. Think about the type of information needed to translate this request into a set of system specifications.

When the data is complete, the description of the change can be translated and expanded into systems terminology. This *translation* minimizes misunderstandings by maintainers.

Systems terminology is the local slang and technical jargon used by system maintainers in relation to the system they support. "User speak" and "systems speak" are often widely divergent.

For example, William Hill of the ACE Co. requested the following change:

> We need an on-line inquiry system to provide data to the customers regarding: back orders, invoices and payments, past orders, and current inventory.

This request might be translated into the following system specifications:

- Create a new sub-system that allows customer inquiries of:

  Accounts Receivable (by client ID, and invoice number)

  Order History (by client ID and order number)

  Back Orders (by client ID and order number)

  Inventory (by part number)
- The Order Entry sub-system has a higher access priority to these data bases. The Inventory Control sub-system has a lower access priority to these data bases.
- This sub-system will be an inquiry-only, on-line system (no update).
- The on-line window for this sub-system will be from 8:00 A.M. to 5:00 P.M., Monday through Friday.
- The screens must be menu driven.
- The data available to the customer must be current to within 24 hours.

CHANGE REQUEST

Identification number: 8602-006

Originator: William Hill—Public Relations

Date originated: 04/01/XX

Date required: 05/01/XX

Type: Adaptive

Severity code: 3

System: Customer Order/Inventory System

Change description: We need an on-line inquiry system to provide data to the customers regarding back orders, invoices and payments, past orders, and current inventory.

Anticipated benefits: Customer satisfaction.
Currently, in order to answer customer inquiries, the service representatives have to read monthly reports (therefore the information is not up-to-date), or call various departments. This process is time-consuming for the service reps and prevents a responsiveness to the client.

Resolution:

Impacts:

  Systems:

  Programs:

  Modules:

  Documentation:

  Hardware:

Phase: Impact analysis

  Phase start date: 02/01/XX

  Approval: Jeff Ridge

  Personnel assigned: Senior technical

  Estimated resources: _____ person days

  Actual resources: _____ person days

Figure 3.3 ACE Co. change request

- The on-line response time must be less than 3 seconds. And there will be up to 100 transactions per hour.
- There will only be one department using the on-line inquiry screens for this sub-system. The maximum number of users at any time will be 12.

After the description of the requested change is translated into systems terminology, the user reviews it for accuracy. When accuracy is confirmed, the impact analysis can be conducted. In this case the user, William Hill, should approve this "translation."

2.2. Hardware Impacts

An impact analysis should also consider the effect of the change on hardware. New hardware may be needed as a result of a proposed change. Changes in processing or the volume of data processed may require the addition of memory, data storage, or teleprocessing hardware.

Based on the ACE system specifications, the following hardware impacts are immediately apparent. They should be noted on the change request.

- Twelve additional terminals.
- Possible CPU upgrade to handle the additional processing and response time.
- Additional telecommunications facilities for 12 terminals.

2.3. System Impacts

The next activity is to determine the impact of the change on existing processes, data stores, data flows, and external entities. The first document to look at is the data flow diagram for the current system.

The system data flow diagram for the ACE Co. is shown in Figure 3.4. Review the system data flow diagram to determine which data bases, processes, data flows, and external entities are affected by the change.

From this data flow diagram, you should see that the requested inquiry system will access the following data bases:

- Accounts Receivable Data Base (DS7)
- Order History Data Base (DS6)

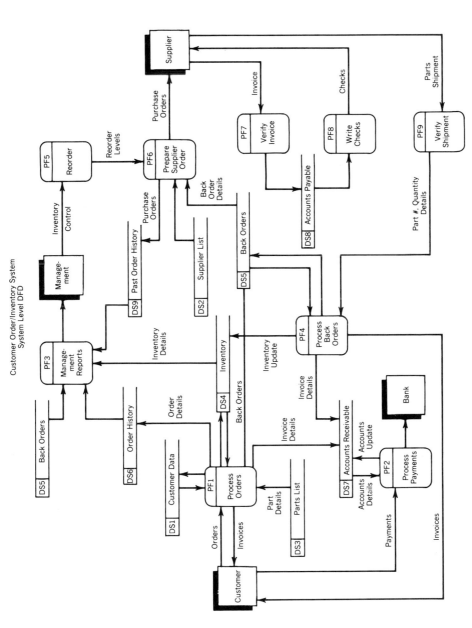

Customer Order/Inventory System
System Level DFD

Figure 3.4 ACE Co. system level DFD (data flow diagram)

49

- Back Orders Data Base (DS5)
- Inventory Data Base (DS4)

The processes potentially affected by the proposed change are:

- Process Orders (PF1 updates Order History)
- Process Payments (PF2 updates Accounts Receivable)
- Management Reports (PF3 accepts data from Back Orders, Order History, and Inventory)
- Process Back Orders (PF4 updates Inventory and Accounts Receivable, while accepting input from Back Orders)
- Prepare Supplier Order (PF6 accepts information from Back Orders)
- Process User Inquiries, a new function will access all of these data stores

All data flows to and from the impacted data bases and processes are potentially affected.

There are no external systems affected by the proposed change. The only external entities are people: customers, management, and suppliers. It is possible that suppliers have a system that accepts data from this one, but no such interface is shown on the diagram.

2.4. Identify Data Impacts

No impact analysis is complete without looking at the data. A complete, up-to-date data dictionary or code library is probably one of the best tools available for determining data impacts. The data dictionary should be analyzed to determine the affected:

- Data items
- Groups
- Structures
- Files
- Data bases

This analysis is particularly important with enhancements because they often involve adding or expanding data fields, which in turn impact every group, structure, file, or data base used by the system.

The analysis is accomplished by scanning the data dictionary or code library using the name of the affected data element. This process will identify all system, program, or module references to that data element.

Also a search can be run on all of the relationships among each affected data element, group, or file. In a properly implemented data dictionary this search will identify every system component impacted by a change to a given field.

If the data dictionary or code library is not current and complete, the analysis will produce incorrect and misleading information.

Even though the ACE change will only read existing data, there may be impacts on existing processes or data. To inquire against the Accounts Receivable Data Base (DS7), Order History Data Base (DS6), and the Back Order Data Base (DS5), the data must be indexed by customer number (ID) and either invoice number or order number. Inquiries against the Inventory Data Base (DS4) need only be indexed by part number.

In this case the maintainer should review the descriptions of the four data bases to see if there are any potential conflicts between the current and required format and organization. The data base descriptions would be found in the data dictionary. If reviewed, the maintainer would find:

- Accounts Receivable Data Base indexed by customer number and invoice number.
- Order History Data Base indexed by order number.
- Back Orders Data Base indexed by customer number and order number.
- Inventory Data Base indexed by part number.

Comparing the output of the data dictionary to the change request description, the maintainer would find that all data bases are indexed properly for inquiry except the Order History Data Base (DS6). It is indexed by order number, not by customer number. Since this data base is not indexed to meet the needs of the inquiry system, the maintainer should access the data dictionary to find out how the Order History Records are laid out. This is shown as follows.

Review the following record and determine how it should be reorganized:

```
Order History Record
    indexed by order_number
    order_number
    customer_number
    number_of_items_ordered
    items_ordered occurs 1 to 100 times
        based on number_of_items_ordered
            item_number
            quantity
            price
```

The Order History Data Base should be reorganized and indexed by order_number *and* customer_number. The record may be changed to place the customer_number first and as the first key into the data base. The revised code would look like the following:

```
Order History Record
    indexed by customer_number and
        order_number
    customer_number
    order_number
        etc.
```

The revision to the data requires that all processes affected will have to be examined further. Note that these processes are Process Orders (PF1) and Management Reports (PF3).

2.5. System Design Explosions

Next the maintainer should review the explosions of the system level data flow diagrams and any written specifications for each process affected.

For example, look at the Process Orders (PF1) data flow diagram shown in Figure 3.5. From this documentation, determine the functions (programs) affected by the ACE change.

Since the Order History Data Base must change, any process that updates or reads the base must be changed. That process is:

Process Valid Orders (PF1.3).

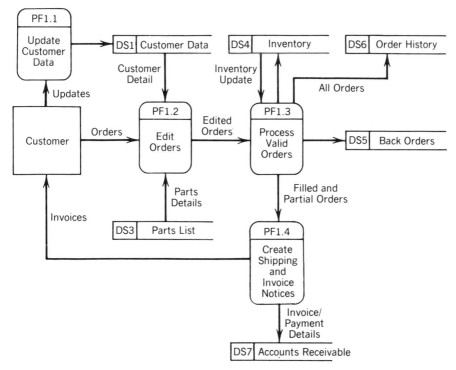

Figure 3.5 PF1—Process Orders DFD Explosion

2.6. Identify Program Impacts

Next the maintainers should review the Process Valid Orders (PF1.3) data flow to determine which functions are affected.

The ACE PF1.3 data flow is shown in Figure 3.6. Review the diagram to determine which functions are impacted.

The affected function is:

Write Order History (PF1.3.1 in Figure 3.6)

Next the maintainer should review the Process Valid Orders structure chart (Figure 3.7) to determine which modules are affected.

You should see that the following module is affected:

Write Order History

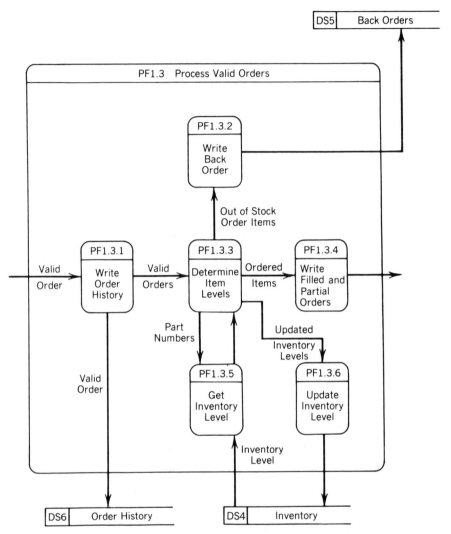

Figure 3.6 PF1.3—Process Valid Orders DFD

2.7. Identify Module Impacts

Finally the module documentation for the Write Order History function should be investigated for its updates of the Order History Data Base. This would include detail on the inputs, processes, and outputs of this module. It would also identify, to the data item level, the data base accesses and updates.

Since the maintainer knows from the change request that the Order

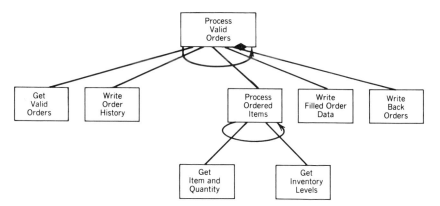

Figure 3.7   PF1.3—Process Valid Orders structure chart

History Data Base is indexed by order_number, and not by cus-
tomer_number, the PDL would need to be updated to reflect that the
orders will be written by customer_number and then order_number.

The following is an example of the revised PDL for the Write Order
History function. The boldfaced material indicates the inserted change.

```
procedure write_order_history(order)
    write order to order_history_database
      indexed by customer_number and
               order_number
end write_order_history
```

2.8.   Documentation

A requested change usually affects documentation throughout the system. All requirements, design, and operational documentation should be
modified to reflect the change. Documentation is often excluded from the
impact analysis, as if it gets updated as a by-product of the maintenance
process. If affected documentation isn't identified and estimated, it won't
be updated.

Take a moment to determine which documents are affected by the
ACE change request:

- System requirements
- System level DFD
- System specifications

- System detailed design documentation
- Update Inventory, Order History, and Back Orders program specifications
- Summarize Order History program design specifications (PF3.3)
- Write Order History module design (PF1.3.1)
- Get Order History Record module design (PF3.3.2)
- Data dictionary
- Inquiry System User Guide (new)

2.9. Human Factors

When software changes, it may be necessary to develop or to change user guides, screen or report layouts, job aids, or work stations. The user's satisfaction with the system is the ultimate test of its usability. Ergonomics, human factors, or whatever you call it, are the backbone of a system's success.

The most important human factors points are where the system interacts with the user:

- Input screens
- Hand and foot controls (e.g., hands on stick and throttle controls in an aircraft)
- Output displays, reports, or sounds
- User and operational documentation
- Computer-aided instruction—tutorials
- On-line help facilities

Take a moment to determine which human factors might be affected by the ACE change.

They are:

- Inquiry screen design
- Response time
- Inquiry selection criteria by customer, item, and so on
- Help screens

2.10.   Identify Other Systems

The impact of a change on other systems is usually found by analyzing design documents and the data dictionary. When an impact on another system is identified, the personnel responsible for the system should be contacted. They will need to conduct a thorough impact analysis of their system.

Once complete, the analyses are used in conjunction with that of the existing system to ensure that all requirements ᵣre met and that post-release corrective maintenance is minimized.

2.11.   Update the Change Request

Finally, the technicians can update the change request with the impacts and resource estimates derived. An updated change request is shown on pages 58–59.

3.   ESTIMATING RESOURCES

This section describes two tools for estimating maintenance resources:

• Function point metrics
• Static analysis/software metrics

It also shows how function point metrics can be applied to the ACE Co. change request used in the previous section.

3.1.   Function Point Metrics

Function point metrics were developed at IBM to help estimate work by counting the number of data flows and interfaces affected by a change. It is applicable to all development and maintenance environments, but *the accuracy of an estimate depends on local productivity figures,* measured as staff days per function point.

A function point is a unit of measurement. It represents the amount of function delivered in a system or program. (Note that a function is some-thing that processes inputs to create outputs.)

To develop a function point measurement, the following steps should be completed:

CHANGE REQUEST

Identification number:	8602-006
Originator:	William Hill—Public Relations
Date originated:	04/01/XX
Date required:	05/01/XX
Type:	Adaptive
Severity code:	3
System:	Customer Order/Inventory System
Change description:	We need an on-line inquiry system to provide data to the customers regarding back orders, invoices and payments, past orders, and current inventory

Create a new sub-system which allows customer inquiries of:

- Accounts Receivable (by client ID, and optional invoice number)
- Order History (by client ID and order number)
- Back Orders (by client ID and order number)
- Inventory (by part number)

The Order Entry sub-system has a higher access priority to these data bases. The Inventory Control sub-system has a lower access priority to these data bases.

This sub-system will be an inquiry only on-line system.

The on-line window for this sub-system will be from 8:00 A.M. to 5:00 P.M. Monday through Friday.

The screens must be menu driven.

The data available to the customer must be current to within 24 hours.

The on-line response time must be < 3 seconds.

There will only be one department using the on-line inquiry screens for this sub-system. The maximum number of users at any time will be 12.

Anticipated benefits: Increased customer satisfaction. Currently, to answer customer inquiries, the service representatives have to read monthly reports (therefore the information is not up-to-date), or call various departments. This process is time consuming for the service reps and prevents a responsiveness to the client.

Resolution:

Impacts:

Systems: Customer Order/Inventory System.
No external systems affected.

Programs: Update Inventory, Order History, and Back Orders (PF1.3)
Summarize Order History (PF3.3)
Process Customer Inquiries (new)

Modules: Write Order History

Human factors: Inquiry screen design
Response time
Inquiry selection criteria by customer, item, etc.
Help screens

Documentation: System requirements
System level DFD
System specifications
System detailed design documentation
Update Inventory, Order History, and Back Orders (PF) program specifications
Summarize Order History program design specifications (PF3.3)
Write Order History module design (PF1.3.1)
Get Order History Record module design (PF3.3.2)
Data dictionary

Hardware: 12 terminals
Possible CPU upgrade to handle additional processing
Additional telecommunication facilities for 12 terminals

Phase: System design

Phase start date: 04/01/XX
Approval: Jeff Ridge
Personnel assigned: Margaux Heitz
Estimated resources: 128 person days
Actual resources: ___ person days

59

- Identify function count elements.
- Develop an initial, unweighted function count.
- Develop total degree of influence.
- Calculate general characteristics adjustment.
- Calculate function points.

Function count *elements* are the basic building blocks of function point analysis. They can be identified from data flow diagrams and consist of the following five inputs and outputs of a system. (The data flow diagram's symbols for each input or output are shown next to each function count element.)

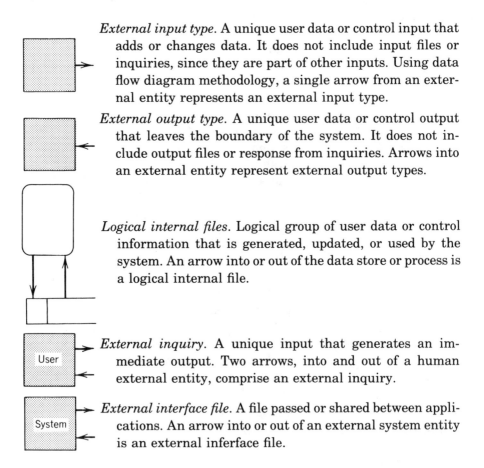

External input type. A unique user data or control input that adds or changes data. It does not include input files or inquiries, since they are part of other inputs. Using data flow diagram methodology, a single arrow from an external entity represents an external input type.

External output type. A unique user data or control output that leaves the boundary of the system. It does not include output files or response from inquiries. Arrows into an external entity represent external output types.

Logical internal files. Logical group of user data or control information that is generated, updated, or used by the system. An arrow into or out of the data store or process is a logical internal file.

External inquiry. A unique input that generates an immediate output. Two arrows, into and out of a human external entity, comprise an external inquiry.

External interface file. A file passed or shared between applications. An arrow into or out of an external system entity is an external inferface file.

Given a system data flow diagram and a description of the required change, a system maintainer should be able to identify all of the impacted

Customer Order/Inventory System
System Level DFD

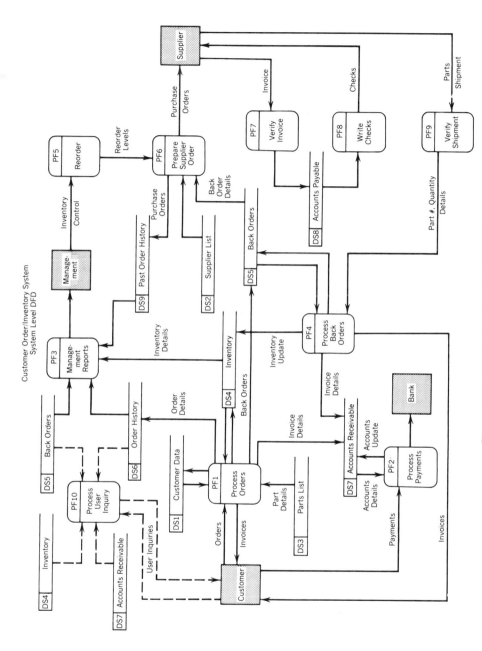

Figure 3.8 Revised system level DFD

61

data flows and therefore all of the basic elements of a function point analysis.

Figure 3.8 shows the revised system data flow diagram for the ACE Co. change request. Review the diagram, and identify the function count elements. They are:

- The six logical internal files (four new and two to the Order History Data Base) of average difficulty (data is logically designed and of medium complexity). The four new internal files are data flows to the new user inquiry function from the four data bases:

    Accounts Receivable Data Base

    Order History Data Base

    Back Orders Data Base

    Inventory Data Base

    Since Order History must change and the data flows that flow from it (from Process Orders and to Management Reports) must be changed, these are the two existing logical internal files.

- There is one external inquiry file (new, from the customer to the new inquiry function) of high difficulty (must handle four different data bases and formats).

- There are no other affected files.

Once the function count elements have been identified, the maintainer should weight the complexity of the change to develop a preliminary function count. Complexity can be rated as low, medium, and high.

An example of a blank function count form follows. There are five rows for the five function count elements and three columns for complexity. The numbers down each column represent the various complexity weights given to each element. These weights are subjective, and they are based on IBM's experience with a wide variety of projects. They are a good starting point for your refinements.

Description	Low	Average	High	Total
External input	__ *3 __	__ * 4 __	__ * 6 __	____
External output	__ *4 __	__ * 5 __	__ * 7 __	____
Logic internal file	__ *7 __	__ *10 __	__ *15 __	____
External interface	__ *5 __	__ * 7 __	__ *10 __	____
External inquiry	__ *3 __	__ * 4 __	__ * 6 __	____
Function count				____

To complete the form, enter the number of low, average, and high complexity function count elements in the cell to the left of the complexity weights. Then multiply the function counts by the complexity weight, and enter the weighted function count in the cell to the right of the complexity weight. When the form is complete, sum the weighted functions across to the right and down into a total function count.

The following is a sample of a completed function count matrix for the ACE example:

Description	Low		Average		High		Total
External input	— *3 —		— * 4 —		— * 6 —		——
External output	— *4 —		— * 5 —		— * 7 —		——
Logic internal file	— *7 —		6 *10 60		— *15 —		60
External interface	— *5 —		— * 7 —		— *10 —		——
External inquiry	— *3 —		— * 4 —		1 * 6 6		6
Function count							66

To account for differences in systems and changes, the summarized function count is then modified. Fourteen system characteristics are used to modify function counts. They are listed here with the associated response for the ACE example:

- Are data communications required? (yes)
- Are there distributed processing functions? (no, existing computer only)
- Is performance critical? (yes, 3 second response time)
- Will the system run in an existing, heavily used operational environment? (yes)
- Does the system require on-line data entry? What is the expected transaction rate? (yes, 100 transactions per hour)
- Does the on-line data entry require the input transactions to be built over multiple screens or operations? (yes)
- Are master files updated on-line? (no update allowed)
- Are the inputs, outputs, files, or inquiries complex? (some, yes)
- Is the internal processing complex? (no)
- Is the code designed to be reusable? (yes)
- Are conversion and installation plans and facilities included in the design? (yes)

- System designed for ease of operation? (yes)
- Is the system designed for multiple installations in different organizations? (yes)
- Is the application designed to facilitate change and ease of use by the user? (yes)

The weights for each characteristic can vary from zero (not present or of no impact) to five (strong impact/influence).

To turn the function count into function points, the maintainer must weight each of the 14 characteristics for each change. The following blank form helps in calculating the total degree of influence these 14 characteristics have:

Characteristic		Characteristic	
Data communications	____	On-line update	____
Distributed functions	____	Complex processing	____
Performance	____	Reusability	____
Heavily used system	____	Installation ease	____
Transaction rate	____	Operational ease	____
On-line data entry	____	Multiple sites	____
End-user efficiency	____	Facilitate change	____

Total degree of influence ____

The sum of these characteristics can modify the function count by ±35% (i.e., maximum weight of $5 \times 14 = 70$) to improve the accuracy of the estimate.

To complete the form, the maintainer should enter a weight from 0 to 5 next to each characteristic. Knowing what weight to assign each characteristic is based on your knowledge of the system and the change. The weights are then summed to derive the total degree of influence the 14 characteristics have.

A completed characteristics form for the ACE example follows. The total degree of influence is 45%, which is 10% above average. This implies that it will take 10% more effort to complete the requested change than normal.

Characteristic		Characteristic	
Data communications	3	On-line update	0
Distributed functions	0	Complex processing	1
Performance	4	Reusability	5
Heavily used system	4	Installation ease	4
Transaction rate	4	Operational ease	4
On-line data entry	4	Multiple sites	3
End-user efficiency	4	Facilitate change	5

Total degree of influence 45

Next a general characteristics adjustment (GCA) should be calculated. Since the adjustment can be ±35%, the initial value must be 65%, and the total degree of influence needs to be added. The formula is:

$$GCA = 65\% + \text{total degree of influence}$$

For the ACE change, the GCA is:

$$65\% + 45 = 110\%$$

Finally, the maintainer calculates the number of function points, using the function count and the characteristics adjustment. The formula is:

$$\text{Function points} = (\text{function count} \cdot GCA)/100\%$$

Using the ACE example of a 66-function count and 110% for a GCA, the function point measurement would be calculated as follows:

$$\text{Function points} = 66 \cdot 1.10 = 72.6$$

In this example, there are 72.6 function points involved in the requested change to the system.

With a little experience and some historical data, this should be an excellent indicator of effort required to make the change. If, for example, it takes the ACE company 1.2 hours to do one function point of work, then it will take 87.1 hours to work the change.

3.2. Static Analysis/Software Metrics

Software metrics is also known as static analysis. It provides quality measurements of the existing program code. These measurements help estimate how much effort will be required to understand a program's function and make the change.

Static analysis looks at size measurements and the complexity of decisions. Three basic measurements of the code describe its complexity:

- Size in executable lines of code (the number of verbs in the code).
- The number of decisions, the complexity of the decision logic—ANDs, ORs, NOTs, and nesting of decisions.

    Decisions are the IF-THEN-ELSE, CASE, DOWHILE, and DOUNTIL statements in every programming language.

    Decision nesting is IFs, CASEs, WHILEs, and UNTILs inside of other IFs, CASEs, WHILEs, or UNTILs.

To understand how decisions affect complexity, take the example of a 50-line FORTRAN program consisting of 25 IF statements in sequence which will have 33.5 million potential control-flow paths (McCabe, *Structured Testing,* IEEE Computer Society Press, 1983).

- The number of GOTOs (these provide the only way to violate structure in most programming languages).

Static analysis, using size and decision complexity metrics, gives a more exact measurement of the underlying code complexity than function point metrics. Such measurement can improve the weights used in the general characteristics adjustment (GCA) portion of function point analysis.

The following characteristics can be measured by static analysis:

- Data communications
- On-line data entry
- On-line update
- Complex processing
- Reusability
- Maintainability

To illustrate how the characteristics can be used, consider:

- Using maintainability as a characteristic for analysis, a highly maintainable module (or unit) of code consists of 100 executable lines of code (ELOC) and fewer than 10 decisions (Arthur, *Measuring Programmer Productivity and Software Quality,* Wiley 1985).

- Using hard-to-maintain programs that are larger than 500 ELOC, and have hundreds of decisions, or dozens of GOTOs. (These programs are also typically less reliable.)

Look at the following static analysis of a COBOL program. You should determine that the program will be difficult to change and give the facilitate-change characteristic a weight of 5:

ELOC	3241	large, complex
Decisions	233	complex
AND, OR, NOT	56	more complexity
Decision complexity	290	test paths
GOTOs	320	structure violations

This program is complex in size, decisions, *and* GOTOs. The complex processing characteristic of the function point metrics should also be 5, which is the maximum influence. For further information on quality analysis, see Arthur, *Measuring Programmer Productivity and Software Quality* (Wiley, 1985).

4. SUMMARY

Impact analysis is a systematic method used to determine the impact of a change on systems, documentation, hardware, telecommunications, and people.

A top-down approach should be used to conduct an impact analysis. Using a top-down approach ensures that all impacts are identified.

The major impact analysis activities are:

- Review change request.
- Translate the change description into systems terminology.
- Obtain user sign-off on the translated specifications.
- Review system requirements.
- Review system design documents.

- Review program design documents.
- Review module design documents.
- Review data dictionary.
- Trace impacts to other systems, documents, hardware, and human factors.
- Develop resource estimates.
- Update change request by documenting the scope of changes and resources required.

Two tools for estimating maintenance resources are:

- Function point metrics
- Static analysis

Function point metrics help estimate work by identifying the data flows, functions, and interfaces affected by a change. It is applicable to all development and maintenance environments, but the accuracy of the estimate depends on local productivity figures.

To develop a function point measurement, the following steps should be completed:

- Identify function count elements.
- Develop function count.
- Develop total degree of influence.
- Calculate general characteristics adjustment.
- Calculate function points.

Function counts are the basic elements of function point analysis. They consist of the following five system inputs and ouputs:

- External input type
- External output type
- Logical internal files
- External inquiry
- External interface file

Static analysis provides quality measurements of program code. These measurements help estimate how much effort will be required to understand the program's function and make the change.

Static analysis looks at size measurements and complexity of decisions. Three basic measurements of code describe its complexity:

- Size in executable lines of code
- Number of decisions, complexity, and nesting
- Number of GOTOs

Static analysis, using size and decision complexity metrics, gives a more exact measurement of the underlying code complexity than function point metrics. These measurements can improve the weights used in the general characteristics adjustment portion of function point analysis.

The following characteristics can be measured with static analysis:

- Data communications
- On-line data entry
- On-line update
- Complex processing
- Reusability
- Maintainability

This chapter has looked at the analysis of impacts and ways to estimate the cost of changes. Performing impact analysis will help you:

- Develop and adhere to a well-defined and structured software maintenance methodology.
- Establish scheduled releases.
- Obtain management's support for software evolution.

The next chapter examines how you use the impact analysis and resulting estimates to schedule a system release. As you will see, proper analysis and estimation will help prevent cost and schedule overruns. Scheduling software releases will help improve productivity and quality as your software continues to evolve.

DISCUSSION QUESTIONS

1. Why don't maintainers perform impact analysis?

2. What are some of the risks of not doing an impact analysis?

3. What are some of the benefits of using a top-down approach for conducting an impact analysis?

4. What are some of the advantages of using function point measurements and static analysis for estimating maintenance resources?

4

System Release Planning

Have you ever been pressured into releasing a program or system prema-
turely, before it was adequately tested? Do you have difficulty finding
time to update design documentation because of those pressures? Does
the user or management ever come to you during maintenance with
revised requirements that cause rework? Do you still catch the blame for
a system failure caused by spurious releases of programs? Scheduled
system releases can cure many of these problems.

An unscheduled system release may get to the program to a user more
quickly, but it may also cause serious problems because of errors resulting from:

• Inadequate design of the change.
• Quick, improper implementation of the change.
• Inadequate testing.
• Improper installation of the revised program.

Not all change requests have the same priority, even though a user
may feel that the changes should be worked immediately. Therefore you

should be familiar with the process of planning what changes to work and when. You should also understand the considerations related to batching changes.

Maintainers and users find it hard to accept the idea of scheduling a system release, although there are extensive benefits to such an arrangement. This chapter looks at the implications of unscheduled and scheduled system releases for maintainer and user productivity and quality.

This chapter also shows how system release planning fits into the overall software maintenance process, provides an overview of system release planning, presents typical problems found when system releases are not planned, describes considerations for batching change requests, and describes the contents of a system release or version description document.

Figure 4.1 shows how system release planning fits into the overall software maintenance process. The diagram in upper left-hand corner shows that system release planning is the third step in the overall software maintenance process.

1. As the exploded diagram shows, system release planning begins by reviewing change requests:

   To help rank (prioritize) changes review description of change and benefits derived.

   To determine resources required for each change, review resource estimates from impact analysis. (This helps determine which changes can be included in the allotted time for each scheduled release.)

2. Change requests are ranked, in priority order, by the user.

3. A technical review board, consisting of users and maintainers, selects the top priority changes for the next release.

4. Change requests are updated with the priority ranking and release number.

5. Changes are batched according to work product to optimize productivity.

6. Management and maintainers plan and schedule the work.

7. Maintainers create a system release or version description document and test plan:

   System release or version description document describes contents and timing of a system release.

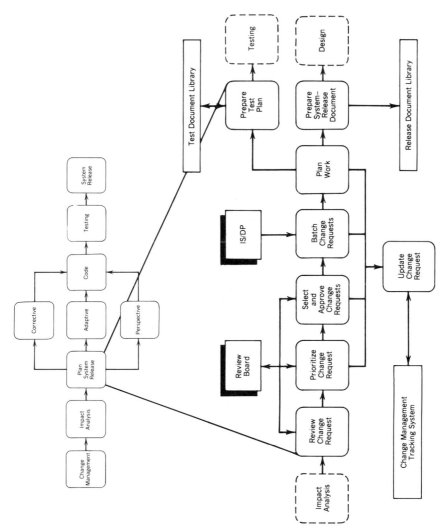

Figure 4.1 System-release planning data flow

Test plan describes how the system will be tested, covering walk-throughs/inspections and computer testing of the changes.

8. The documents are entered into the documentation libraries section of the configuration management system.

9. Change requests are passed to design, coding, and testing personnel for implementation.

1. RELEASE PLANNING

This section describes the risks associated with unscheduled system releases, the concept of scheduled system releases, and the benefits of its use. Finally, an approach for batching changes to improve productivity is explained.

As described in the preface, a consistent, repeatable process is the third phase of software engineering maturity. Scheduled releases and release planning are essential to achieving this third level of maturity. The basic objectives of system release planning are to:

- Establish a schedule of system releases.
- Determine the contents of a system release.

Contrast these objectives to the chaos that ensues whenever change requests are worked individually and the revised products are released immediately. Unscheduled releases cause confusion because:

- Maintainers assume that all changes are of equal priority. The most important, revenue-generating ones may fall back in the first-in/first-out (FIFO) queue, delaying business opportunities.
- Users can't schedule training and documentation revisions to coincide with the release.
- The released product may be unreliable. Testing of the changes is spotty and inadequate; only unit or integration testing can be accommodated. System testing is difficult, if not impossible, because running an entire system test takes time and planning, which are in short supply when releases are unscheduled.
- Operators are unprepared to implement and run the new release.

To avoid such problems, maintainers should implement scheduled releases.

1.1. Scheduled Releases

The practice of scheduling system releases (i.e., monthly, quarterly, semiannually, or annually) reduces the risks associated with working changes as they are requested. Some other benefits of scheduling system releases are that this:

- Improves productivity by allowing the users to rank their changes and have the maintainers do the most important ones first.
- Improves productivity because changes affecting specific programs can be worked at the same time, instead of independently (batching concept).
- Focuses work, and aids in developing schedules and allocating resources. Because releases are scheduled in advance, change requests can be allocated to a particular release based on its priority. This practice also facilitates controlling the work.
- Improves quality because there is time to design changes to "fit" in with the existing design, and because releases can be evaluated by an independent quality assurance group.
- Results in better test data and more adequate testing. System testing is cost-effective in a scheduled environment. Scheduling releases enables test planning to begin before the designs or code are changed. Early test planning is a key to effective testing and a high-quality product.

Planning a system release to achieve these benefits involves the following activities:

1. Rank all changes in a priority order (user).
2. Select the top-ranking changes that can be done with the available personnel and resources (user and maintainers). This information is available from the impact analysis estimates.
3. Secure user agreement on the contents and timing of a system release.
4. Obtain approval to implement the proposed changes.
5. Schedule work in groups, by work product, to maximize productivity of users, maintainers, and managers.
6. Prepare a system release document.
7. Prepare a test plan.

1.2. Batching Changes

When change requests have been ranked, selected, and approved by the users, maintainers can batch them by system, sub-system, data structure, program, and module.

Batching change requests minimizes the time a maintainer spends learning the design or code for each change. Maintainers can do multiple changes to one module more easily than when each change is done separately.

For each change, and for each maintenance activity (i.e., design, code, and test), the maintainer must:

- *Learn* the existing design, code, or test material.
- *Determine where and how* to make or test the change.
- *Make* the change, *develop* new test data, and *test* the change.

By batching changes, the first two steps are done only once for all changes that affect the design, code, or test data.

Figure 4.2 shows how seven change requests (each arrow represents a change request) that affect one system might be batched for implementation. Information about all affected components comes from the *impact section* of the change request. This information was gathered during the impact analysis.

In this example a top-down approach is used to batch the change requests. First, the changes are batched by affected system (seven changes for this system) and sub-system (four for sub-system *A* and three for sub-system *B*). Managers might assign this system level design work to different analysts for implementation.

Second, all changes that impact the data design are batched and assigned to a data administration group to design the new data structures.

Third, changes are batched by program and module. Batching changes by program and module makes it easier to manage the work in program design, module design, coding, unit (module) testing, and integration (program) testing. This helps managers and project leaders tell when the project gets off schedule.

After module design, the code is written and unit tested. (Unit testing is covered in Module 9.)

Some additional items to consider when batching changes are:

- Schedules and personnel availability.
- Knowledge of application.
- Knowledge of skills needed for each phase of the change.

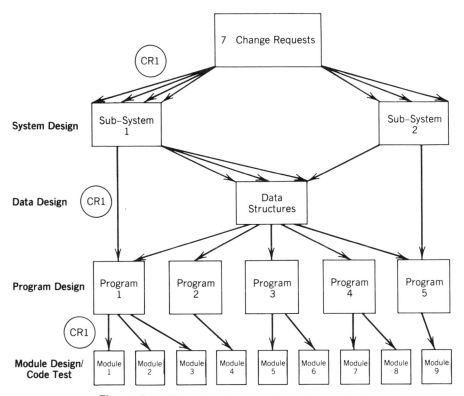

Figure 4.2 Batching changes by work product

Once the changes have been ranked, selected, and batched for a scheduled release, maintainers create a system release or version description document (DOD) to describe the forthcoming release.

2. SYSTEM RELEASE/VERSION DESCRIPTION DOCUMENT

This section describes the function of a system release or version description document, which identifies the contents and timing of a system release. It also serves as a communication device between maintainers and users of the system.

Maintainers prepare a system release or version description document as the system release plans are developed. The document is revised throughout the design, coding and testing phases of maintenance.

Since the release document evolves over the course of a release, it can be used to further improve communications between users and maintainers by:

- Serving as a first draft of the contract between the user and maintainers for a revised product.
- Serving as a description of the system release to aid installation and operation.
- Serving as a blueprint for changes in training and user documentation.

A system release or version description document can also be used by the operations center (or whoever runs the software) as requirements for hardware upgrades and the development of installation and operational procedures.

A system release document can be as simple as a binder of change requests for the system release, or it can separate this information into a more usable package. This package should include change request numbers, descriptions, list of all programs and documents changed, and a system overview.

The contents of the system release document might include the following:

- Cover letter and table of contents
- Overview of system release

    Major enhancements (scope)

    Release delivery and installation dates

    Approximate schedule for design, code, and test
- Specific products listed on the impact analysis

    Programs affected

    Data, files, and data bases affected

    Design, operation, or user documentation
- List of change requests to be included in the system release (version description class I and II changes)
- Notes pertaining to the release
- Appendixes and attachments of relevant documents

Without a system release document, there is no means of communicating between maintainers and users who implement the software release. They need to know about the release to:

- Plan for its implementation.
- Allocate resources for conversion and implementation.
- Develop backout procedures in case of a system failure.

Without a system release document as a guide, these steps are not possible, meaning that they will either be done poorly, causing system problems, or will delay the implementation of the software.

Two sample system release documents follow. Notice that the samples differ in content and level of detail. The first is an example of a business-oriented payroll system release. The second is a DOD standard DID for a Version Description Document which is partially complete.

SAMPLE RELEASE DOCUMENT

System Release Document
for the
Payroll System
Release 3, 1986
March 15, 1986
Prepared for:
Department/Contracting Agency
Prepared by:
Department/Contractor

SAMPLE RELEASE DOCUMENT (continued)

Table of Contents

Description	Page Number
Overview of the system release	Page X
Specific products	Page X
Documents	Page X
Programs	Page X
Notes	Page X
Appendixes	
Payroll System Job Control Language Library	Appendix A
Payroll System Data Base Library	Appendix B
Distribution Listing	Appendix C
Payroll System Data Base Design	Attachment 1
Payroll System Operations Guide	Attachment 2
Payroll System User's Guide	Attachment 3
Payroll System Run Guides	
PA02	Attachment 4
PA05	Attachment 5
PA20	Attachment 6
Change requests included in release	Attachment 7

SAMPLE RELEASE DOCUMENT (continued)

Overview of the   This System Release Document describes Re-
system release: lease 3, 1986, of the Payroll System. The major
                         enhancements contained in this release include:

Change Request No.	Description
8602-001	Zip code increase from 5 to 9 digits
8602-004	Name field increase to 30 characters
8602-009	Payroll code addition

Schedule: Payroll System Schedule—Release 3, 1986:

System Test Start Date:	March 20, 1986
Acceptance Test Start Date:	April 1, 1986
Release Date:	April 15, 1986
Installation Date:	April 20, 1986

Specific products: Employee Data Base Design   Attachment 1
Documents: This attachment describes all of the changes
                            made to the Employee Data Base and any op-
                            erational considerations caused by the
                            changes.

                         Payroll System Operations Guide   Attachment 2
                            This attachment describes the changes to the
                            Payroll System Design and any operational
                            considerations caused by the changes.

                         Payroll System User's Guide   Attachment 3
                            This attachment describes changes to the user
                            or client procedures.

                         Payroll System Run procedures:
                            Run procedures are included in the System
                            Release Document to identify all operational
                            revisions by program caused by the release;
                            e.g., additional files that need to be processed,
                            JCL changes for a program, different error
                            condition handling procedures.

SAMPLE RELEASE DOCUMENT (continued)

PA02	Attachment 4
PA05	Attachment 5
PA20	Attachment 6

Payroll System Design

Programs: Payroll Program and module designs for the following programs:

Programs Released	Release Date	Install Date	Operational Changes
PA01	04/15/86	04/20/86	No
PA05	04/15/86	04/20/86	Yes
PA15	04/15/86	04/20/86	No
PA02	04/16/86	04/21/86	Yes
PA20	04/20/86	04/30/86	Yes

Change requests: Release 3 change requests   Attachment 7
List of all changes included in release 3.

Notes: A conference will be held to discuss Release 3, 1986 of the Payroll System on April 1, 1986, at 10:00 A.M. in Room 66 of the Galleria Bldg.

All questions or concerns regarding Release 3, 1986 of the Payroll System should be directed to the Project Manager on (212) 555-5555.

Appendixes: Payroll System Job Control   Appendix A
Some organizations build production JCL and include it when the programs are transmitted to production.

Payroll System Data Base   Appendix B
Usually the Production Data Bases are created and transmitted to the production sites with the programs as a complete library.

Document Distribution Listing   Appendix C
The distribution listing helps keep track of all the affected parties in a System Release and assists the communication process.

SAMPLE VERSION DESCRIPTION DOCUMENT

Version Description Document
for the
X-22 Heads Up Display (HUD)
CONTRACT NO. GS123-456
CDRL SEQUENCE NO. 19.1
March 21, 1986
Prepared for:
Static Dynamics
Prepared by:
Heads Up, Inc.
1 Cranium Drive
Marblehead, MA

SAMPLE VERSION DESCRIPTION DOCUMENT (continued)

Table of Contents

1. Scope
2. Referenced documents
3. Requirements
4. Notes
5. Appendixes

SAMPLE VERSION DESCRIPTION DOCUMENT (continued)

1. SCOPE

1.1. Identification

This Version Description Document describes Version 21 for the CSCI identified as the X-22 Heads Up Display System (X22HUD) 19.1.

1.2. Purpose

The purpose of this system is to collect data from all of the weapons, navigational, and radar systems on the X-22 as well as all of its sensors and project this information onto the canopy of the X-22 so that the pilot will not need to look down to see the instruments. The major functions:

- Gather airspeed, attitude, and navigational information.
- Gather and update weapons and target information.
- Display this information on the HUD.

This version includes map modes for the HUD display and the correction of several defects that caused the HUD display to freeze in flight.

1.3. Introduction

This document will describe the new release of the X-22 HUD system, including all applicable documents, hardware and software requirements, quality controls, testing processes, and overall objectives.

2. REFERENCED DOCUMENTS

2.1 Government Documents

SPECIFICATIONS

    System/Segment Specification
    Software Requirements Specification
    Interface Requirements Specification
    Software Product Specification

STANDARDS

    MIL-STD-2167
    Software Standards & Procedures Standard

DRAWINGS

    TBD

OTHER PUBLICATIONS

    TBD

SAMPLE VERSION DESCRIPTION DOCUMENT (continued)

2.2. Nongovernment Documents
3. VERSION DESCRIPTION
3.1. Inventory of Materials Released
3.2. Inventory of CSCI Contents
3.3. Class I Changes Installed
3.4. Class II Changes Installed
3.5. Adaptation Data
3.6. Interface Compatibility
3.7. Bibliography of Reference Documents
3.8. Operational Description
3.9. Installation Instructions
3.10. Possible Problems and Known Errors
6. NOTES
Appendix I

3. SUMMARY

The basic objectives of system release planning are to:

- Establish a schedule for system releases.
- Determine the contents of a system release.

System release planning activities include the following:

- Review change requests.
- Rank change requests (user).
- Select and approve change requests (user).
- Batch change requests.
- Plan work.
- Prepare system release document and test plan.

System releases can be scheduled or unscheduled. An unscheduled release can cause problems with:

- Doing the most important changes first.
- Scheduling training and documentation revisions to coincide with the release.
- Adequate testing of the change.
- Implementing and running the new release.

A scheduled release is the method of working changes, typically dozens or hundreds at a time, so that work can be managed like a development project. Some benefits of scheduling system releases are:

- Improved productivity
- Improved quality
- Improved planning and control

Batching change requests by system, sub-system, data structure, program, and module optimizes resource allocation and maintainer productivity. Batching change requests minimizes the time a maintainer spends learning the design or code for each change.

Once changes are batched, maintainers create a system release or version description document that describes the contents and timing of a system release. Since the release document evolves over the course of the release, it can be used to improve communications between users and maintainers by:

- Serving as the first draft of a contract between the user and maintainers for a revised product.
- Serving as an outline of the system release, for those changing or installing any part of the system.
- Serving as a blueprint for changes in training and user documentation.

The critical success factor that system release planning addresses is establishing scheduled releases and batching change requests.

This chapter described the release planning process, benefits of planning system releases, and considerations for batching change requests. It also described the contents of a system release and version description documents.

The next chapter describes techniques for performing corrective maintenance, which can either be scheduled or unscheduled (emergency).

DISCUSSION QUESTIONS

1. Why do maintainers and users resist scheduling system releases?

2. What are some of the risks associated with working changes as they come in?

3. What would you tell management or users to help convince them of the importance of scheduled releases?

4. What are some of the factors that should be considered when batching change requests?

CHAPTER

5

═══

Corrective Maintenance

It's a bleak Thursday. Everything that can go wrong has. You've worked 10 hours on a fix for a program that blew up in production. You come home, drink a beer, eat a TV dinner or order a pizza. You're ready for a quiet night bouncing around among the network's prime-time offerings, when the boss calls to have you fix a program that just blew up and its not even yours. Harry's on vacation and somebody has to fix it. Armed with an inadequate description of the problem and no contact to question, you march off to fix it. After a few minutes of trying to interpret the available incoherent nonsense, a wave of panic fills your mind as you wonder what to look for, how to look for it, and where to start.

The aim of this chapter is to provide you with the knowledge and tools to answer the three questions of what to look for, how to look for it, and where to start. This chapter:

- Describes a process for performing corrective maintenance.
- Explains a technique that assists you in defining problems.
- Describes a process for developing and testing hypotheses about the causes of the problem.

1. CORRECTIVE MAINTENANCE CONCEPTS

This section provides an overview of the activities involved in identifying and correcting software defects.

Corrective maintenance includes all repairs of defects in an existing system. Corrective maintenance ensures that a system continues to perform as specified in the requirements.

Defects refer to any problems with the system's hardware, software, or documentation. For example, corrective maintenance is needed when:

- A program fails or aborts.
- A program produces results that do not match the software requirements.
- A hardware component, such as an I/O processor or disk drive, fails, causing a system failure.
- The software documentation—requirements and designs—does not match the software it supports.
- The user documentation—operation or user guides—misleads the user into activities that cause incorrect results or system failures.

The preceding problems can stem from:

- Requirements specification errors. For example, the user incorrectly specified the system's functions.
- Design errors resulting from misunderstood change requests, software requirements, or design specifications; inconsistent, convoluted, or complex logic; and large, unmodular systems. As high as 80% of all problems stem from the requirements and design of software (Arthur 1983).
- Coding errors resulting from misunderstood design specifications, incorrectly implemented design specifications, or faulty code logic.

Repairing defects has its own set of problems. Two prevalent ones are:

- Cleanly repairing a defect. Repairing a defect has a significant (20–50%) chance of introducing another defect. And the percentage increases when one line of code, or more than 10 lines of code are involved in the change. So the entire process can be thought of as "two steps forward and one step back" (Brooks 1975).

- Increased testing. Because every change seems to create new defects, corrective maintenance requires more testing per statement than any other programming.

There are two factors behind the failure to repair defects cleanly. First, a defect surfaces as a local failure of some kind. However, it often has nonobvious systemwide implications; attempts to repair the defect with minimal effort will repair the obvious, but the ripple effect may be overlooked. Second, the person who makes the repair is generally not the person who wrote the code.

The consequence of these two factors is that *every solution causes new problems*. Without a comprehensive method for fixing defects that anyone can use, more bugs will be injected into the system causing additional corrective maintenance (fixing a bug in program 2 causes program 3, downstream, to fail; once program 3 is corrected, it causes program 4 to fail, etc.).

This module presents a general method for fixing defects. Before it is described, we need to define two types of corrective maintenance.

Basically, there are two types of corrective maintenance:

- Emergency repairs
- Scheduled repairs

1.1. Emergency Repair

If a missile guidance system does not accurately track its programmed course, it is defective and needs repair. Likewise, if a payroll system fails to produce paychecks for all employees, the software must be repaired. These situations require *emergency repair* (Figure 5.1). Emergency repairs include all severity 1 and 2 defects, (see Chapter 2).

Usually emergency repairs are performed within short time frames. Thus there is little regard for careful design and integration of the changes. In addition emergency repairs often focus on a single program. However, the changes may impact the entire system, as well as downstream systems.

Therefore emergency repairs must eventually loop back to the start of the software maintenance process and be treated as a new change request. Reexamining an emergency repair in a scheduled release will ensure that the repairs are correctly implemented and the documentation updated.

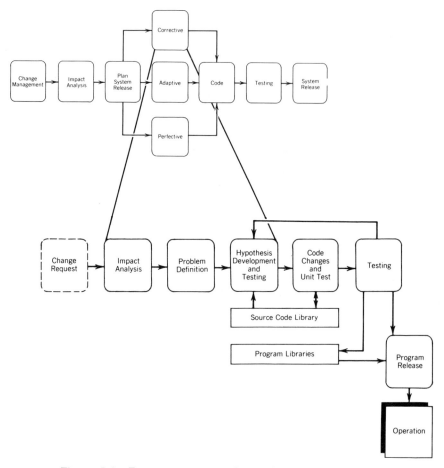

Figure 5.1   Emergency corrective maintenance data flow

1.2.   Scheduled Repairs

Scheduled corrective maintenance is used to:

- Fix defects that do *not* require immediate attention.
- Reexamine all emergency repairs.

Defects that do not require immediate attention are corrected within the context of a scheduled system release (Figure 5.2). Defects of this nature are generally severity 3 and 4 (see Chapter 2). Some examples of defects that might be classified as scheduled repairs are:

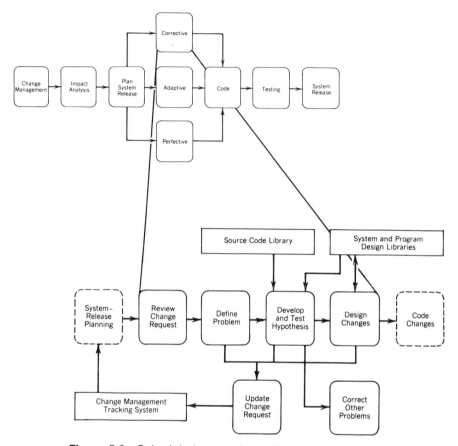

Figure 5.2 Scheduled corrective maintenance data flow

- A defect that produces incorrect results in a noncritical component can be handled in a scheduled release. For example, an incorrect result in a data analysis routine should be fixed in a scheduled release.

- In a redundant embedded real-time system, the failure of mission critical software component (e.g., the fire control system) may demand an emergency repair. The fix, conducted at a remote site, such as an aircraft carrier at sea, should be reexamined back at the maintenance site in a scheduled release.

To determine if a defect warrants emergency repair status, ask the following types of questions:

- Does the defect endanger human life?

  For example, a defect in autopilot software that adversely affects landing in poor visability, or a radar system that fails to spot wind shears.

- Will the defect cause a significant number of people to be unproductive?

  For example, an inoperative, large on-line system is intolerable because of the thousands of users made nonproductive, or an airline reservation system that loses revenue with each hour of downtime.

- Does the defect impact financial operations?

  For example, a billing system that stops producing bills and thus halts the flow of revenue.

- Did the defect cause the system to go down or crash?

If the answer is "yes" to one or more of these questions, then emergency repair is necessary.

2. PROBLEM SOLVING

An ideal technique for finding and correcting defects is to use a problem-solving process. The best problem solvers go through the following activities to find and fix problems:

1. Define the problem, looking for clues about the origin of the problem. Even the absence of information is often a clue.

2. Develop hypotheses about the cause of the problem. Based on your experience, apply heuristics (rules of thumb) to the possible causes of the problem.

3. Eliminate as many hypotheses as possible, and select the most likely ones for testing.

4. Select a strategy for testing the problem based on the hypothesis (i.e., top-down, bottom-up, fan-in, fan-out).

5. Test each hypothesis, discard it, or use it to correct the problem.

2.1. Review the Change

Before analyzing the problem, you need to understand the requested change. The pitfalls of not doing this are that you may solve the wrong problem, or implement the wrong solution. When reviewing the change request, look for clues and missing, unclear, or extraneous information. The change request for this example is shown in Figure 5.3.

CHANGE REQUEST

Identification number: 8602-007

Originator: William Hill—Public Relations

Date originated: 04/01/XX

Date required: 06/01/XX

Type: Corrective

Severity code: 2

Problem origin:

   System: Customer Order/Inventory System

   Program: Unknown

Change description: Based on an audit of customer invoices, the Customer Sales Management Report is incorrectly summarizing the sales for each customer. The report totals are always lower than the audit. This is causing inventory shortages, increased back orders, and lost revenue.

Anticipated benefits: Increased revenue and customer satisfaction by having the right amount of inventory at the right time.

Resolution:

Impacts:

   Systems: Customer Order/Inventory System

   Programs:

   Modules:

   Documentation:

   Hardware: None

   Telecommunications: None

Figure 5.3 ACE Co. change request

2.2.   Define the Problem

Based on the change request, problem solvers define the problem by addressing the following parameters:

- *What* the problem is and is not.
- *Where* the problem occurred and did not occur.
- *When* the problem occurred and did not occur.
- What the *scope* of the problem is and is not.

Defining the negative side of the problem often provides as many clues as defining what the problem is.

2.3.   Problem Analysis Matrix

Using these parameters, maintainers can develop a problem analysis matrix to illustrate the problem graphically. The problem analysis matrix created from the example change request is shown in Figure 5.4.

PROBLEM DEFINITION MATRIX

	IS	IS NOT
WHAT	Invalid sales totals by customer consistently low	Any other totals; higher than audit
WHERE	Management Sales Reports	Other management reports or any other reports (i.e., Inventory/Billing Reports)
WHEN	Apparently all of the time only detected by audit	Before last audit
SCOPE	Occurs with all customer sales totals	Only part or a few of the customer sales totals

Figure 5.4   Problem definition matrix for ACE Co. problem

3. HYPOTHESIS DEVELOPMENT

To develop hypotheses about the cause(s) of a problem, start with the problem statement (change request) and the problem definition matrix. They provide clues about the origin and causes of the problem.

Also use the following tools to identify likely causes of the problem:

- System and program design documents and specifications
- Source code listings
- Program inputs and outputs
- Compiler cross-reference listings
- Linkage editor listings and storage maps
- Execution monitors

To localize the potential cause(s) of the problem, consider four areas:

- *Hardware.* Which piece of hardware is out of commission or operating abnormally (i.e., CPU, disks, memory, tape, telecommunications network, input/output BUS)?
- *Documentation.* Is incorrect operational documentation causing the operator to do something that makes the system fail or deliver incorrect results? Is incorrect user/customer documentation causing data entry problems that result in processing errors?
- *Operator/Operations Error.* Did the operator forget (or refuse) to read the operating instructions? Did the operator fail to install the new version of the program?
- *Software.* Which data, files, or data bases are accessed? Which programs use or create the data? Which programs and data are upstream from the point the problem was detected?

When working on a software problem, knowing the major types of defects and their frequency of occurrence is invaluable. Knowing which defects occur most frequently helps focus the analysis and development of hypotheses.

Table 5.1 lists the major software defects and their frequency of occurrence. The statistics are based on the research of Lopow (1979), Mendis, and Craig (1974).

As you review the data, notice that the major sources of errors are:

TABLE 5.1   Defect Potential by Type

Defect Type	Lipow	Mendis	Craig	Total
Logic	26%	38%	16%	25%
Computational	9	24	19	40
Interface	16	20	16	56
Data manipulation	18	10	16	70
I/O	14	4	19	85
Data base	10	0	10	95
Other	7	4	4	—

- Logic (decisions)
- Computations $(+, -, /, \star)$
- Interfaces (between modules)
- Data manipulation $(a = b)$

These areas should be the initial focus of hypothesis development. Also the cumulative percent column shows that 95% of all errors fall into the first six categories. The following are examples of these major types of defects.

Logic   Logic errors involve:

        Taking the wrong action following a decision:

           IF A > B   IF A > B

             MAXIMUM = B   MAXIMUM = A

        Wrong decisions:

           IF DAY = 31   IF DAY = 31 AND

             DO END OF MONTH   MONTH = JAN,

                                 MAR, etc.

        Looping too many or too few times

           WHILE angle < 90   WHILE angle <= 90

Computational   Computational errors include:

        Incorrect data (i.e., FED-TAX = GROSS-PAY $\star$ STATE-TAX-RATE)

        Incorrect operators (i.e., Replace multiplication sign $(\star)$ with addition)

Interface   Interface errors occur when the data passed from one module to another is converted, truncated, or mutated.

Data
Manipulation

Data manipulation errors occur when:

Receiving fields are shorter than sending fields (i.e., move 1000 into a field only three digits in length—the computer chops off the "1" and leaves the zero)

Data fields are not initialized before using them (e.g., setting numeric fields to zero and alphabetic fields to blanks)

Input/Output

Input/output errors occur when:

Working in input/output buffers. Data should be read into or written from static working storage that does not change as records are read or written.

Data Base

Data base errors occur when the:

Data base is updated incorrectly.

Data base is corrupted by hardware problems.

Data base is restored from the wrong backup copy.

Other

Other errors include:

Transmission problems

System software problems (i.e., operating system problems)

The next step is to rank order each hypothesis. Rank ordering should start with the most likely and end with the least likely. The rank depends on all of the clues you've assembled to this point. Testing the most likely hypothesis first and then the remaining ones shortens the problem-solving process.

4. HYPOTHESIS TESTING

Next test the hypotheses using one of the following approaches: top-down, bottom-up, fan-in, or fan-out. Remember more than one approach may be needed to find the source of the problem.

4.1. Top-Down

Maintainers apply top-down hypothesis testing when there are no obvious clues about where to start (i.e., you don't precisely know where to begin looking for the cause of the problem). Begin by understanding the physical design of the program and what the code does. Use the structure chart to identify functions that might have incorrectly modified the field in error. If documentation doesn't exist, create it. A visual representation of the program assists in locating the source of a defect. Mechanical documentation generators can create structure charts from existing code.

Once likely candidates are identified, move to the code for verification, following the field from the time it enters the module until it leaves the module (i.e., passed to another module or written out). Look for potential defects.

The tools used in top-down testing are change requests, problem definition matrix, source code listings, and system and program design documents and specifications.

4.2. Bottom-Up

Maintainers follow a bottom-up testing process when you know the symptoms of the problem. Begin where the incorrect field was created or updated and work backward, looking for the typical types of errors listed earlier. Continue working backward until the source of the defect is found; many times it will reside in other programs or configuration items.

The tools used in bottom-up testing are the change request, problem definition matrix, and source code listings.

4.3. Fan-Out

Maintainers fan out when the bottom-up approach fails. Start with the incorrect field, and use a compiler cross-reference listing to find every statement that modifies the data field under investigation. Continue until the source of error is found.

Tools used are the change request, problem definition matrix, source code listings, and compiler cross-reference listings.

4.4. Fan-In

Maintainers fan in when bottom-up and fan-out fail. Start with where the data enter or leave the system/program and work in from the boundaries of the software.

4.5. Other Methods

4.5.1. Examine Input Data. Examine input data using a file or data base dump utility and/or an on-line browse facility. This is most useful when the hypothesis is that garbage-in has created garbage-out, or a program failure.

Tools used are change request, problem definition matrix, and source code listings and program inputs and outputs.

4.5.2. Trace Execution. Best application is when the logic is so complex that it cannot be followed. Traces show execution flow, typically by label, within a program. The problem with traces are that the output is so voluminous that it often obscures the defect instead of illuminating it.

Tools used are change request, problem definition matrix, source code listings, on-line debugging tools, and linkage editor listings and storage maps.

4.5.3. Analyze Execution. Use an execution analyzer, which shows how many times each statement in the code was executed. Execution analyzers find loops executed one too many, or too few times, and a host of similar code problems.

Tools used are change request, problem analysis matrix, and execution monitors.

4.6. Debugging Tips

A checklist of tips for debugging programs follows. These tips are especially useful when you get close to a problem but can't quite see it.

- Think about and mentally analyze the problem.
- Describe the problem to a co-worker. In the process of explaining the problem, you often uncover it.
- If you hit a mental block, take a walk—rhythmic exercise seems to shake problems loose. If possible, sleep on the problem—a lot can happen overnight.
- Use the computer as a last resort. Trial and error rarely solves the problem.

4.7. Testing Guidelines

Some guidelines for testing hypotheses are:

- Exclude unlikely hypotheses and tests.
- Test most likely hypothesis first, and then subsequent ones.
- Isolate one error at a time, but don't assume that fixing the first error will solve the problem.
- Use available debugging tools.
- Embed debugging code into the program and test the existence of the defect and its correction.
- Know where the most errors occur in a given program. Defects tend to cluster in small portions of the code; look there first.

5. PROBLEM RESOLUTION

Once a cause hypothesis is tested by human inspection and confirmed, the defect can be repaired. Defect repair occurs by changing the code to:

- Fix logic errors.
- Correct computational statements.
- Use the right data in operations.
- Manipulate the data correctly.
- Correct the program's input or the previous program's output.
- Fix the data base.

5.1. Repair Tips

Fixing a bug can be harder than finding it. Making it stay fixed can be tricky. Use the following tips to maximize your chances for success:

- If you find a roach in your motel room, you'd say the place was *infested*. Look for other defects around the code you're correcting.
- Fix the defect, not the symptom. For example, if a total is consistently three low, don't just add three to the total. Find out why those three are missing from the total.
- When you fix a defect, odds are good that you've also created a new one. Use regression testing to weed out any new errors.

- The odds of correcting code the first time decrease as the size of the code increases. Complex programs can be extremely difficult to debug and repair. Budget extra time to test changes to complex programs.

  Once corrected, the code is inspected (as described in Chapter 8) and tested (as described in Chapter 9). Unfortunately, not all defects are simple one-line changes. Often there are multiple causes for the defect, and correcting one part of the problem will cause other defects to surface during testing. "Don't stop with one bug." Continue testing and debugging until all causes of the defect have been identified and eliminated.

6. HYPOTHESIS DEVELOPMENT AND TESTING EXAMPLE

This section walks through an example of hypothesis development and testing. It describes the key things to think about when developing and testing hypotheses about the cause(s) of software defects.

6.1. Hypothesize Causes

After the problem is defined, a hypothesis about the cause(s) of the problem is developed and tested. Developing a cause hypothesis is similar to debugging a newly developed program.

The key difference is that during maintenance, the system has been thoroughly tested and is in operation. Therefore the defect must be one that was not anticipated by any of the test cases used to verify the system. This defect may have a combination of causes that are harder to detect.

6.2. Hypothesis Development

To develop a cause hypothesis, start by reviewing the change request, problem analysis matrix, and system design documents to determine which processes, data stores, data flows, and external entities might contribute to the problem.

The change request (Figure 5.3), problem analysis matrix (Figure 5.4), and data-flow diagram for the current system (Figure 5.5) are used to develop hypotheses about the problem. Review the problem description (on the change request) and the problem analysis matrix. Then look at the data flow diagram and determine the most likely source of the problem.

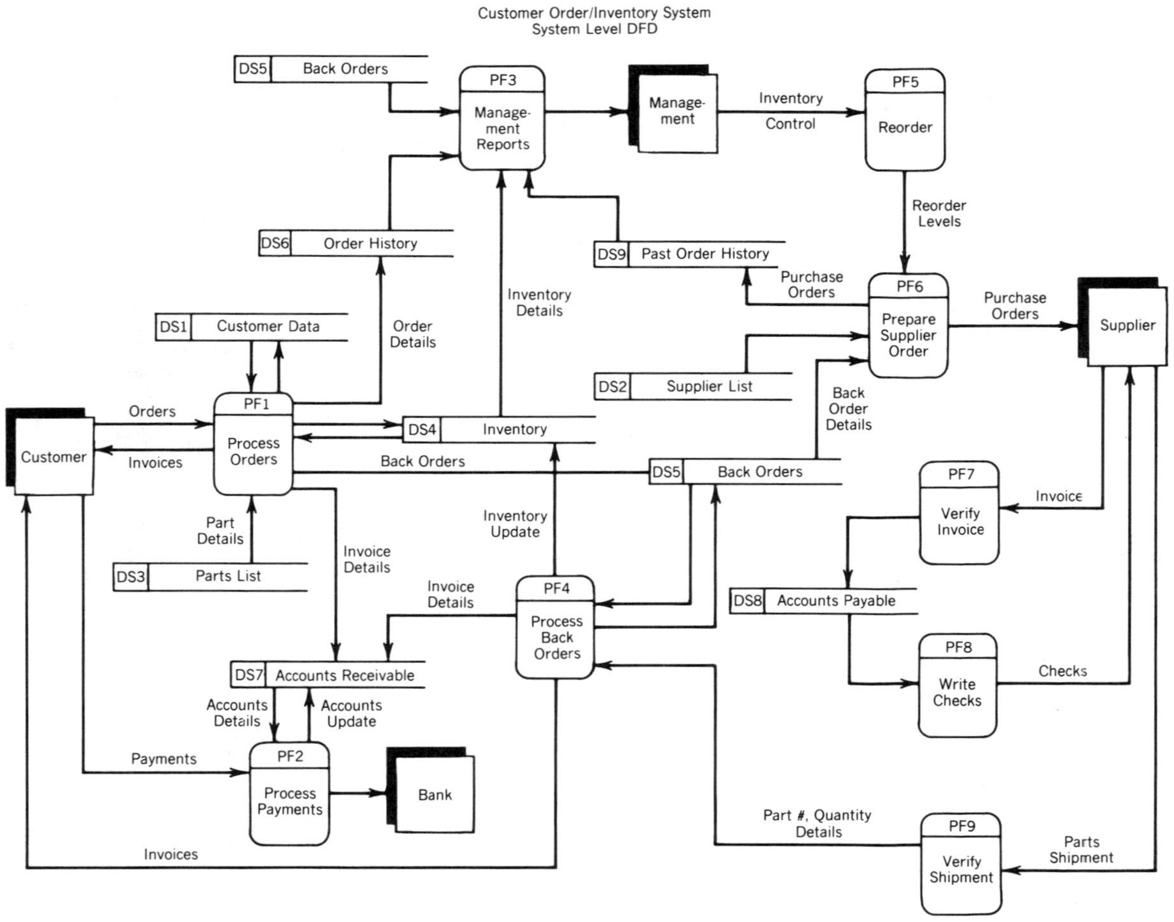

Customer Order/Inventory System
System Level DFD

Figure 5.5 ACE Co. system DFD

From this data flow diagram you should develop the following hypotheses:

- The most likely source of the problems is in the Management Reports process (PF3). Why?

    Because the output to the external entity—management—is incorrect. Therefore either the processing of PF3 or one of its inputs—Inventory (DS4), Back Order Data Base (DS5), Order History Data Base (DS6), Accounts Receivable Data Base (DS7)—is flawed.

    Knowing that the most common defect is in the logic, and not the data, the first hypothesis should be investigated until it proves correct or incorrect.

- One of the inputs to PF3 is incorrect.
- The auditor's findings are incorrect, and management has made poor buying decisions.

    The likelihood of this hypothesis being correct is very remote. So it will only be tested as a last resort.

Next you should review the explosions of the system data flow diagram and any written specifications for each process affected to determine which program generates the sales reports.

Take a moment and look at the Management Reports explosion shown in Figure 5.6. Determine which program generates the sales reports, and develop additional hypotheses based on your findings.

The Summarize Order History (PF3) program generates the sales reports.

From this diagram the following hypotheses can be made:

- The processing in Summarize Order History is working incorrectly. This can be tested by working through the code.
- The input from Order History is incorrect. This can be tested by examining the data. If the data is incorrect, look at the system data flow diagram to determine which process creates the Order History Data Base. That process is PF1 (Process Orders). One of the programs in PF1 may be incorrectly creating the data base. This can be tested if the Order History Data Base is found to be incorrect.

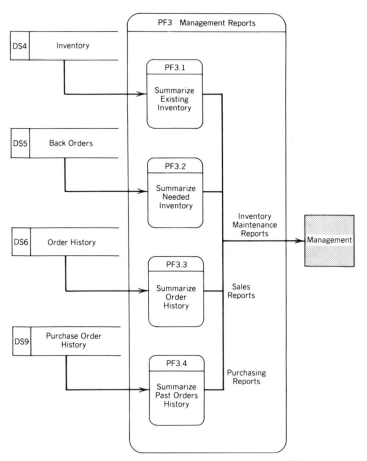

Figure 5.6   PF3—Management Reports DFD

Next review the structure charts for all modules that access the Order History Data Base or summarize sales by customer. The structure chart of "Summarize Order History" is shown in Figure 5.7. Review the chart and determine which module should be further analyzed.

The structure chart shows that the "Accumulate Sales by Customer" module should be reviewed for potential processing problems.

Finally, the code for the "Accumulate Sales by Customer" module should be examined for logic or calculation problems that could have caused the defect. Review the code for the Order History Record and the "Accumulate Sales by Customer" that follow, and see if you can find the problem:

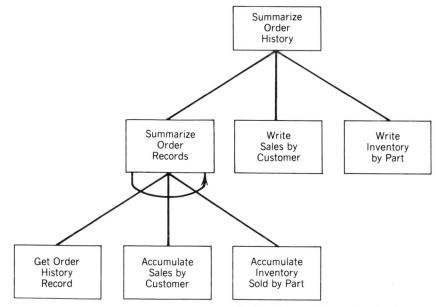

Figure 5.7 PF3.3—Summarize Order History hierarchy chart

• Order History Record:

```
Order History Record
    indexed by order_number
               customer_number
               number_of_items
    items_ordered occurs 1 to 100 times
        based on number_of_items
          item_number
          quantity
          price
```

• Accumulate Sales by Customer:

```
Procedure accum_sales(order_record)
    item_index = 1
    while(item_index < number_of_items)
      customer_sales(customer_number) =
        quantity(item_index) *
          price(item_index)
```

```
        item_index = item_index + 1
    endwhile
end accum_sales
```

Knowing that one of the most common problems with loops and indexes is not performing all iterations of the loop, look at the conditional statement in the "while" loop. Note that *not* all the iterations can be processed. The final item is missed—when the item_index equals the number of items. This causes all sales summaries to be low. To test the hypothesis, the one line of code should be changed to read as follows (note that bold faced material indicates the change):

```
while(item_index <= number_of_items)
```

Knowing that bugs tend to cluster, never stop with the first bug. Take a moment and look for any other defects.

Knowing that the problem deals with sales calculations, look at the statement that calculates the sales totals by customer. You should find the other error.

Each calculation *replaces* the previous one, rather than accumulate the total. To fix the module completely, the code should be changed as follows:

```
procedure accum_sales(order_record)
    item_index = 1
    while(item_index <= number_of_items)
        customer_sales(customer_number) =
            customer_sales(customer_number) +
            quantity(item_index) *
                price(item_index)
        item_index = item_index + 1
    endwhile
end accum_sales
```

Having survived this analysis and human testing, the code can be computer tested. The last step is to update the change request. A revised change request is shown in Figure 5.8.

CHANGE REQUEST

Identification number: 8602-007

Originator: William Hill—Public Relations

Date originated: 04/02/XX

Date required: 06/01/XX

Type: Corrective

Severity code: 2

Problem origin: Accumulate Sales by Customer module

   System: Customer Order/Inventory System

   Program: Summarize Order History

   Module: Accumulate Sales by Customer

   Type of error: Logic—not processing all iterations of loop
Computation—not correctly accumulating totals

Change description: Based on an audit of customer invoices, the Customer Sales Management Report is incorrectly summarizing the sales for each customer. The report totals are always lower than the audit. This is causing inventory shortages, increased back orders, and lost revenue.

Anticipated benefits: Increased revenue and customer satisfaction by having the right amount of inventory at the right time.

Resolution: Correct the "Accumulate Sales by Customer" module to process every item number (i.e., it stopped one short every time). And correct accumulation computation to add to, instead of replace, the customer totals.

Impacts:

   System: Customer Order/Inventory System

   Program: Summarize Order History

   Module: Accumulate Sales by Customer

   Documentation: None

   Hardware: None

   Telecommunications: None

Figure 5.8   Revised ACE Co. change request

7. SUMMARY

As described in this chapter, the purpose of corrective maintenance is to fix defects in the existing software. Corrective maintenance ensures that the system operates as specified in the requirements. Corrective maintenance frequently involves correcting requirements, design, and coding errors.

There are two types of corrective maintenance:

- *Emergency corrective maintenance* which is used to fix defects that require immediate attention.
- *Scheduled corrective maintenance* which is used to fix defects that do *not* require immediate attention and to reexamine all emergency repairs.

A similar process is used to resolve each type of corrective maintenance. The primary difference is that emergency corrective maintenance is a compressed version of the scheduled corrective maintenance process. Because emergency repairs must be made quickly, they should loop back through the scheduled corrective maintenance process to ensure proper implementation.

Corrective maintenance cannot be entirely eliminated—to err is human. However, using the following techniques can substantially reduce it:

- Scheduled releases
- Structured design and coding techniques
- Fault tolerant designs and coding techniques
- Use of automated debugging tools
- Quality assurance audits
- Defect analysis

Defects are found and resolved by a three step process:

1. Problem definition
2. Hypothesis development
3. Hypothesis testing

Problem definition describes the problem in terms of what, where, when, and the scope of the problem. The why and how of the problem are

left for hypothesis development and testing. It is often useful to describe these four characteristics not only in terms of what they are, but what they are not. Knowing what the problem cannot be helps eliminate many potential hypotheses.

The major hypothesis development and testing steps are:

- Review the problem definition.
- Localize the problem to a particular area, such as hardware, documentation, operator/operations, or software.
- Develop a list of hypotheses starting with the common defects—logic, computational, data, I/O, etc.
- Rank order each hypothesis in terms of likelihood.
- Test the hypotheses in rank order.

Use one of the following approaches to test hypotheses:

- Top-down. Use the structure chart to identify functions that might have incorrectly modified the field in error.
- Bottom-up. Begin where the incorrect field was created or updated, and work backward, looking for the typical types of errors discussed earlier in this reading.
- Fan-in. Start from the boundaries of the software, and work in following the input or output.
- Fan-out. Start with the incorrect field, and use a compiler cross-reference listing to find every statement that modifies the data field under investigation.
- Trace the execution.
- Use a dynamic analyzer to find logic problems.

This chapter addressed the following critical success factors:

- Use of structured design and coding principles.
- Introduction and use of modern, automated tools to improve quality and productivity.

This chapter described a process for performing corrective maintenance work—correcting defects. The next chapter looks at a process for designing enhancements to change the functionality of existing software.

DISCUSSION QUESTIONS

1. What are some of the difficulties you have when correcting defects?

2. What are some of the risks of not reexamining emergency repairs?

3. Brooks characterized software maintenance as taking two steps forward and one step back. What actions can be taken to minimize the impact of fixing defects?

4. What if the code for the "Accumulate Sales by Customer" module was correct. What would be your next hypothesis, and how would you test it?

5. What if your next hypothesis was incorrect also. Then what would you do?

CHAPTER

6

=====

Adaptive Maintenance

Most people have been taught how to develop new systems, but not how to maintain or enhance the old ones. Managers often put new programmers on development in the mistaken belief that these green troops can build maintainable, flexible software. It is not possible. Maintenance is the best training ground for learning how *not* to build software. Adaptive maintenance is the best place to learn how to design and build small, flexible enhancements to a working system and, in the process, learn a lot about how to build large systems correctly, from the ground up.

Adaptive maintenance is a process used to enhance the functionality of software, hardware, and their documentation. Enhancements add, change, or delete functions from existing programs or systems.

The purpose of this chapter is to:

- Familiarize you with the concepts of adaptive maintenance.
- Describe the process of adaptive maintenance.
- Describe the system, program, and module design processes involved in adaptive maintenance.

115

Enhancements can rarely be worked without considering the system, programs, and modules involved. Failure to look at the impact of the change at every level typically results in an increasingly complex, inflexible, unmaintainable, and unreliable system. This in turn causes rewrites or replacement of the system.

Therefore each maintainer should review the change request, impact analysis, system release document, and design documents to understand the impacts of the change. The major pitfall of not fully understanding the change is that you create a system that the user doesn't want or that works contrary to the user's needs.

To avoid these problems, the major adaptive maintenance steps (shown in Figure 6.1) are:

- Requirements definition
- Data design
- System design
- Program design
- Module design

Requirements	Review the change request to understand the new or changed requirements. The change request should clearly identify:
	Affected inputs
	Affected outputs
	Affected processing functions and algorithms
	Implementation constraints
	Available resources
	Then the requirements document should be updated to reflect any changes, and a requirements walk-through conducted to ensure accuracy.
System Design	System design work determines where and how to implement system level changes. System level data flow diagrams and their explosions are used to determine the existing processes, data stores, data flows, and external entities that need revision.
Data Design	Any changes to the data—including data bases, files, structures, groups, or elements—are designed. The design should comply with naming conventions and

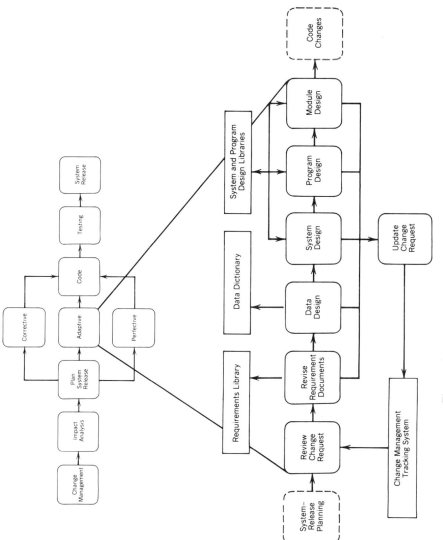

Figure 6.1 Adaptive maintenance data flow

117

minimize the impact of the data change. All affected data are updated in the data dictionary, and new data layouts, files, or data bases are created.

System and data design are typically performed at the same time.

Program Design	Program design documents are analyzed to determine where to add, change, and delete functions to implement the requested change.
Module Design	Module design documents are analyzed to determine how to integrate changes into an existing module, create a new one, or delete an existing function.

1. ADAPTIVE MAINTENANCE

This chapter defines adaptive maintenance. It describes the factors that invoke it. It also explains the similarities between adaptive maintenance and new development.

Adaptive maintenance begins when an *enhancement* change request is approved. The objective of adaptive maintenance is to evolve any system to meet the needs of the user and business.

To meet these needs, the adaptive maintenance process augments the functions of software, hardware, and documentation. Maintainers adapt software whenever they add, change, or delete functions from existing systems, programs, or modules. For example, adding a new mode to a surveillance radar is an enhancement, and so is changing vendor data in an inventory control system.

By meeting these goals and objectives, many benefits are derived from adaptive maintenance:

- Increased revenues by improved responsiveness to business opportunities.
- Improved productivity by automation of manual activities and performing computations that cannot be done reliably by hand.
- Increased customer satisfaction.

Several factors may invoke adaptive maintenance:

- Internal needs
- Competition
- External requirements

Internal needs include automating existing manual functions, such as a billing system. Internal needs may also include expanding existing systems or changing a system to accommodate new methods and practices. One such example might be the conversion of payroll processing from monthly to bimonthly or weekly.

Competition refers to other companies who have similar systems that have been enhanced. For example, airline A and airline B both have reservation systems. Airline A does not offer seat assignments through travel agents. Airline B can. This feature would prompt more than one customer to use airline B over A.

External requirements might include enhancements mandated by law (federal, state, or local). Such changes are not negotiable. For example, consider laws covering minimum wages and social security.

Adaptive maintenance is essentially the same as new development. The main differences are that changes are integrated into an existing design and the time lines are shorter.

Integrating changes into an existing design is trickier than developing an entirely new design because the architecture and design of an existing system are typically cast in spaghetti code. Any new functionality should adapt to the current structure. Maintainers who use structured design and programming practices make their job more like new development by designing new modules for inclusion in existing programs.

Enhancements can rarely be worked without considering the system design and the subsequent program and module levels. Failure to design the change at each level can result in an increasingly complex, unmaintainable, and unreliable system. This causes rewrites (replacement) of the system or higher maintenance costs.

Like the development phase of software design, adaptive maintenance should be done using structured design principles. Top-down design minimizes the difficulty of integrating new functions into an existing system; new functions are designed as independent modules. This practice minimizes changes to the existing system and allows the new function to be designed with reusability, maintainability, and other qualities in mind (see MIL-STD-2168). Structured design can also decrease the cost of maintenance while making programs easier to maintain.

In summary, adaptive maintenance includes all work related to changing the functionality of the software. Adaptive maintenance is generally performed because of new or changing requirements.

Adaptive maintenance is much like new development when structured design principles are followed. Using top-down design minimizes the impacts on the existing system. New modules and programs can then be designed, with reusability and maintainability in mind, to provide the expanded capability.

2. REQUIREMENTS DEFINITION

The enhancement change request contains a description of the revised capability desired by the customer or client. Either the client or the maintainer must examine the change and fit it into the existing system requirements. If the change doesn't fit the existing system design, then perhaps it should be developed separately as a new system rather than implemented as a kludge in the existing one. This is the earliest point at which you can detect potential problems in the implementation of the system.

3. SYSTEM DESIGN

This section walks through an example of how to perform system and data design. The example is an enhancement to add an on-line function that supports customer inquiries.

Each maintainer should perform the following system design activities covered in this reading:

- Understanding the change.
- System design:

    Identify affected data bases and processes.

    Evaluate design alternatives.

    Update system-level design documentation.

    Review exploded data flows.

    Update lower-level design documentation.
- Data design:

    Identify affected record layouts.

    Design the changes.

3.1. Review Change Request

The first step is to review the change request and understand the scope of the change, implementation constraints, and available resources. The pitfall of not doing this is that you create a system the client doesn't want.

On the following pages is a change request received by the data processing department at ACE Auto Parts. This example builds on the ACE example used in Chapter 3.

Review the following change request to familiarize yourself with the change and to identify each of the following:

- Inputs affected
- Outputs affected
- Processing affected and changes in algorithms
- Constraints on implementation of the change
- Resources available

CHANGE REQUEST

Identification number:	8602-006
Originator:	William Hill—Public Relations
Date originated:	04/01/XX
Date required:	05/01/XX
Type:	Adaptive
Severity code:	3
System:	Customer Order/Inventory System
Change description:	We need an on-line inquiry system to provide data to the customers regarding back orders, invoices and payments, past orders, and current inventory

Create a new sub-system that allows customer inquiries of:

- Accounts Receivable (by client ID, and optional invoice number)
- Order History (by client ID and order number)
- Back Orders (by client ID and order number)
- Inventory (by part number)

The Order Entry sub-system has a higher access priority to these data bases. The Inventory Control sub-system has a lower access priority to these data bases.

This sub-system will be an inquiry only on-line system.

The on-line window for this sub-system will be from 8:00 A.M. to 5:00 P.M. Monday through Friday.

The screens must be menu driven.

The data available to the customer must be current to within 24 hours.

The on-line response time must be < 3 seconds.

There will only be one department using the on-line inquiry screens for this sub-system. The maximum number of users at any time will be 12.

Anticipated benefits:	Increased customer satisfaction. Currently, to answer customer inquiries, the service representatives have to read monthly reports (therefore the information is not up-to-date), or call various departments. This process is time-consuming for the service reps and prevents a responsiveness to the client.
Resolution:	
Impacts:	
Systems:	Customer Order/Inventory System No external systems affected.
Programs:	Update Inventory, Order History, and Back Orders (PF1.3) Summarize Order History (PF3.3) Process Customer Inquiries (new)
Modules:	Write Order History Get Order History
Documentation:	System requirements System level DFD System specifications System detailed design documentation Update Inventory, Order History, and Back Orders (PF) program specifications Summarize Order History program design specifications (PF3.3) Write Order History module design (PF1.3.1) Get Order History Record module design (PF3.3.2) Data dictionary
Hardware:	12 terminals Possible CPU upgrade to handle additional processing
Telecommunications:	Additional telecommunication facilities for 12 terminals
Phase:	System design
Phase start date:	04/01/XX
Approval:	Jeff Ridge
Personnel assigned:	Margaux Heitz
Estimated resources:	128 person days
Actual resources:	_____ person days

The following points, mainly from the description and impact analysis, should be noted about the change request:

- Inputs:

  Customer Inquiry
  Accounts Receivable   (by client ID and invoice number)
  Order History   (by client ID and order number)
  Back Orders   (by client ID and order number)
  Inventory   (by part number)

- Outputs:

  Order History (updated by Process Orders)

  Inquiry Response

- Processing:

  Create a new on-line sub-system that allows customer inquiries into the four data bases.

  The screens must be menu driven.

  There will only be one department using the on-line inquiry screens for this sub-system. The maximum number of users at any time will be 12.

- Constraints:

  The on-line window for this sub-system will be from 8:00 A.M. to 5:00 P.M. Monday through Friday.

  The data available to the customer must be current to within 24 hours.

  The on-line response time must be < 3 seconds.

- Resources:

  Date required (one month) is out of line with the estimated time and personnel assigned to the project. Either more personnel are needed, or the time line needs to expand.

3.2. Review System Design

Now review the system design documents to determine existing data bases, processes, and external entities that need to be revised. The first document to look at is the data flow diagram for the current system (Figure 6.2).

Take a moment to review the system data flow diagram to determine

Customer Order/Inventory System
System Level DFD

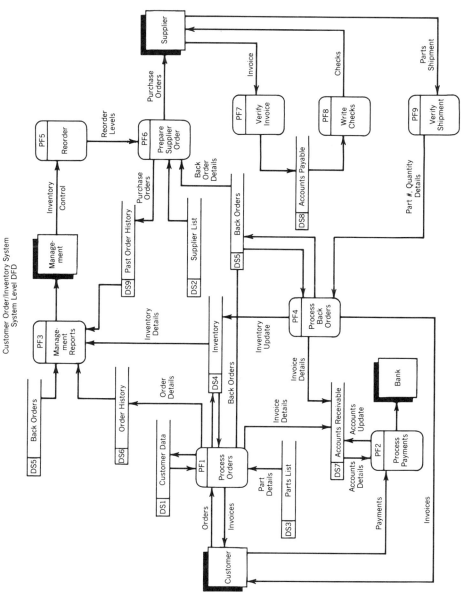

Figure 6.2 ACE Co. system data flow

125

which data bases, processes, and external entities are affected by the change.

From the data flow diagram, you should see that the requested inquiry system will access the following data bases:

- Inventory (DS4)
- Back Orders Data Base (DS5)
- Order History Data Base (DS6)
- Accounts Receivable Data Base (DS7)

The processes affected by the change are:

- Process Orders (PF1 updates Order History)
- Management Reports (PF3 reads Order History)

The external entity affected by the change is "CUSTOMER."

The next activity is to evaluate various design alternatives. There are a couple of approaches to designing this enhancement: merge the inquiry function with processing orders or create a separate sub-system.

Merging the inquiry function with Process Orders (PF1) seems possible since PF1 accesses or updates all of the required data stores. However, this option would reduce the flexibility and maintainability of the system because:

- Processing Orders and Processing User Inquiries are not compatible activities. Trying to merge them could complicate the design and code.
- Looking further, PF1 updates Order History, Back Orders, and Accounts Receivable. It does not, however, read these data bases (arrows into PF1 from these data bases), so new logic would be needed to process user inquiries.
- Looking at the explosion of PF1 (Figure 6.3), notice that two programs, PF1.3 and PF1.4, control the Order History (DS6), Back Orders (DS5), and Accounts Receivable (DS7) data bases. These are probably both batch processes, and only the Edit Orders (PF1.2) function is on-line. This means that programs PF1.3 and PF1.4 need to be modified to on-line programs that can read the data bases. This change would probably require a complete rewrite.

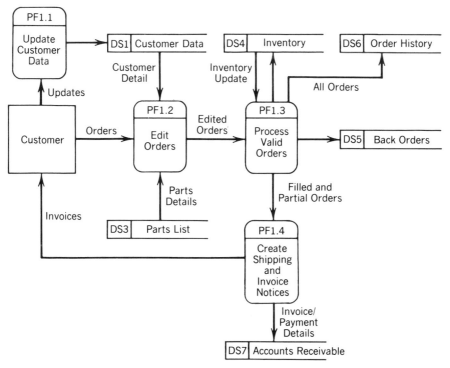

Figure 6.3 PF1—Process Orders DFD

The second alternative is to design a new function—Process User Inquiries (PF10)—that will access all of these data stores. This alternative has several advantages:

- The new function can be designed using a structured methodology.
- There are few impacts on existing processes or data because the change only reads existing data. Only the data flows to and from the Order History Data Base and its connected functions are affected because of the change in indexing.

Faced with massive changes to two programs or writing a new program to handle the inquiries and only minor changes necessary to existing programs, a maintainer should chose the second solution.

The next activity is to update the system data flow and design specifications to reflect the chosen design alternative. To do this, begin with the affected external entity and connect it to any new processes.

The proposed design is shown in the upper left-hand corner of the revised system data flow diagram (Figure 6.4). The affected external entity is CUSTOMER. The entity CUSTOMER should be attached to a new process bubble with two arrows—an inquiry function. The new process should be labeled Process User Inquiry (PF10).

Next update the data flow to show connections to the four data bases. Since two of these would require difficult connections, Inventory (DS4) and Accounts Receivable (DS7), the data bases are reproduced in the upper left-hand corner of the diagram.

The new process can be designed and built separately, as a development project. The remainder of this section will describe the remaining changes to the existing system, not the new design.

The next activity is to review explosions of the system data flow diagram and any written specifications for each process function affected. This documentation is used to design the required changes.

Review the following data flow explosions to determine which processes are affected.

- Process Orders (PF1), shown in Figure 6.3
- Management Reports (PF3), shown in Figure 6.5.

From the data flow diagrams and impact analysis, a maintainer would determine that the following processes are affected by the change in the Order History Data Base:

- Process Valid Orders (PF1.3)
- Summarize Order History (PF3.3)

Because of the selected system design alternative, there is nothing to update on these diagrams. There will, however, be updates to the written system specifications (not shown here) and the subsequent program and module design documents.

Having identified all of the affected system data flows, the next activity is to design the data, on those data flows, for ease of processing.

4. DATA DESIGN

Data design includes changes to the data including: data bases, files, structures, groups, and elements. The designer updates all affected data in the data dictionary and creates new data layouts, files, and data bases.

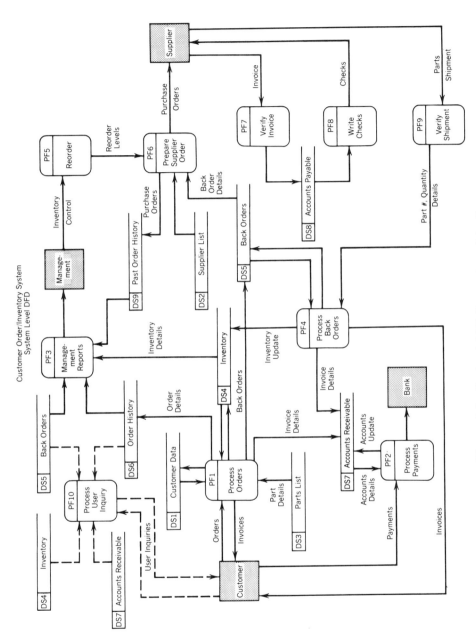

Customer Order/Inventory System
System Level DFD

Figure 6.4 Revised ACE Co. system data flow

129

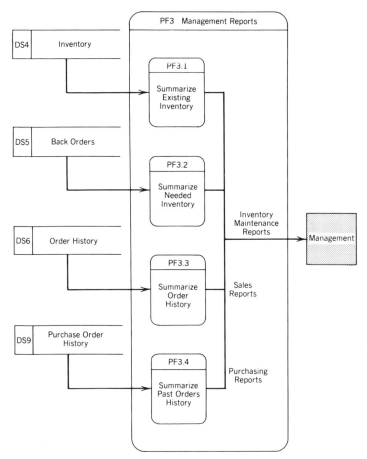

Figure 6.5 PF3—Management Reports DFD explosion

Data design should be done by a data base designer to ensure compliance with naming standards and to minimize the impact of data changes.

Data base designers apply canonical modeling tools to change the data design, inserting the new data fields and restoring the design to third normal form—all *nonkey* data items are fully, functionally dependent on the *primary key* and independent of each other (e.g., in an employee record, employee name and salary are both dependent on the employee's SSN, but not on each other).

A complete up-to-date data dictionary is probably one of the best aids available for performing data design. A good data dictionary will carry common names for a data element, such as order_number. Also it will reference all possible data bases and processing of that data element.

For the ACE Co. enhancement example, the first activity is to review the description of all affected data in the data dictionary. In this example the description of the Order History Data Base (DS6) would read as follows:

Order History Data Base indexed by order number.

By comparing this description with the change description section of the change request, you should notice that the Order History Data Base is not indexed to meet the needs of the inquiry system. The descriptions of the other affected data bases would show that they are already indexed properly for the inquiry function.

Next the data dictionary should be accessed to see how the Order History Records are designed. In the ACE example the records are laid out as follows:

```
Order History Record
    indexed by order_number
  order_number
  customer_number
  number_of_items_ordered
  items_ordered occurs 1 to 100 times
    based on number_of_items_ordered
    item_number
    quantity
    price
```

From this layout the maintainer would notice that the Order History Data Base (DS6) should be reorganized and indexed by customer_number (primary key) *and* order_number. The record would be changed to place the customer_number first and as the first key into the data base.

These changes would look as follows (the boldfaced material denotes changes):

```
Order History Record
    indexed by customer_number and
      order_number
```

customer_number

order_number

number_of_items_ordered

items_ordered occurs 1 to 100 times

   based on number_of_items_ordered

   item_number

   quantity

   price

Having properly determined the data and system design, the design work can continue at a program and module level.

5. PROGRAM DESIGN

This section builds on the last one by walking through an example of how to perform program and module design. The ACE Auto Parts Co. example is again used to illustrate the points. The major activities covered are:

- Program design:

   Identify affected modules.

   Design changes.

- Module design:

   Identify affected code.

   Design changes.

- Conduct design walk-through.

- Update documentation, including the resolution section of the change request.

5.1. Update Program Design

During program design, design documents and structure charts are reviewed to determine where functions need to be added, changed, or deleted.

At the system level maintainers are focusing on the logical view of the design. At a program and module level they shift to a physical implementation of the logical design. This is why structure charts, written specifi-

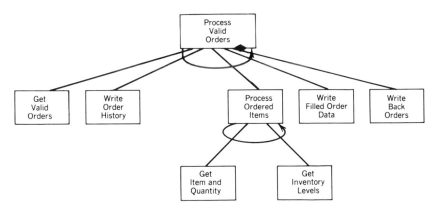

Figure 6.6   PF1.3—Process Valid Orders structure chart

cations, and pseudocode play a stronger role in documenting the program and module designs.

In the ACE example recall that the affected programs are Process Valid Orders (PF1.3) and Summarize Order History (PF3.3); see exploded diagrams of Process Orders (PF1, Figure 6.6) and Management Reports (PF3, Figure 6.7).

Look at the structure charts to determine the modules that access the Order History Data Base. These modules, and possibly any that access them, will need to be changed. From the structure charts the maintainers would determine that the Write Order History and Get Order History Record modules are likely candidates for change.

The proposed design for this part of the enhancement is:

- Change the Write Order History to use the new Order History record, and write it, indexed by customer number and order number. It can accept the information from the calling module in the previous interface format and write it out in the new format. This is a classic example of information hiding.
- Change the Get Order History Record module to read the new Order History record by customer and order number. Reformat the information, and pass it to the calling module. This is also a classic example of information hiding and data coupling.

Both of these modules will have functional strength—they perform a single, simple function.

Since there are no changes to either the program data flow diagrams or

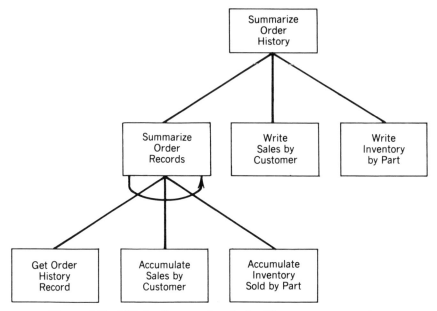

Figure 6.7   PF3.3—Summarize Order History structure chart

structure charts, the maintainer would update the written program specifications to reflect the changes in the Order History Data Base and its access.

5.2.   Update Module Design

During module design, maintainers decide how to integrate the necessary changes into an existing module, create a new module, or delete an existing function.

Module design begins by reviewing the documentation for the affected modules identified during program design. In the ACE example those would be the Write Order History and Get Order History Record modules.

When reviewing the documents, look at how the modules access the Order History Data Base (DS6), and determine what changes need to be made and how. The following shows the pseudocode or program design language for the two modules:

```
procedure write_order_history_record(
     order_number, customer_number,
     number_of_items, items_ordered)
```

```
        write order to order_history_database
        indexed by order_number

    end write_order_history

    procedure get_order_history_record(
        order_number, customer_number,
        number_of_items, items_ordered)

        get order from order_history_database
        indexed by order_number

    end get_order_history
```

Notice that the code is incorrect. Both modules should be indexed by "customer_number" and "order_number." The revised code for each module would look as follows (the boldfaced material denotes changes):

```
    procedure write_order_history_record(
        order_number,  customer_number,
        number_of_items,  items_ordered)

        write order to order_history_database
        indexed by customer_number and
                    order_number

    end write_order_history

    procedure  get_order_history_record(
        order_number, customer_number,
        number_of_items, items_ordered)

        get order from order_history_database
        indexed by customer_number and
                    order_number

    end get_order_history
```

From this you might ask why such simple routines are not included in the main module. Answer: To isolate the processing from the data base. Also, they can be reused.

The final activity is to update all design documents and the change request. Once updated, the documents are stored in the configuration management system to ensure that all data are controlled. Maintainers then update the change request in the change request tracking system to ensure that all changes are documented and complete.

The resolutions section of the ACE example change request could be updated as follows:

1. Change the Order History Data Base to be indexed by customer _number (primary key) and order_number (secondary key). Reorganize the data base to reflect the change in the data structure.

2. Revise the Write Order History module in program Update Inventory, Order History, and Back Orders (PF1.3.1).

3. Revise the Get Order History Record module in Summarize Order History (PF3.3).

4. Recompile other modules using the new Order History data layout.

5. Design an entirely new function and one or more programs to inquire from the four data bases.

6. DESIGN GUIDELINES

A number of guidelines should be followed during design:

- Minimize the impact on existing systems by changing as little as possible of the existing system and adding new programs or modules.
- Look at alternative designs to find one that is compatible with the existing design. This minimizes effort and future maintenance costs.
- Choose a design that maximizes the use of *reusable* modules.
- Choose a design alternative that maximizes modularity.
- Choose a design that minimizes the effect on system quality.
- Choose designs that are easily testable.
- Choose designs that maximize the usability of the system.
- Hide (i.e., put in unique modules) functions likely to change from

other processing to improve maintenance. This is Parnas's "information hiding" technique (Parnas 1979).

- Modularize around sources of change to minimize future maintenance.
- Require a minimum amount of worker effort.
- Require a minimal use of worker memory.
- Minimize worker frustration.
- Maximize use of the existing habit patterns.
- Maximize tolerance for human differences.
- Maximize tolerance for environmental changes.
- Provide prompt problem notification when a worker makes an error.
- Allow maximum worker control of tasks.
- Provide maximum support for worker tasks.

7. SUMMARY

Adaptive maintenance is a process used to enhance the functionality of software, hardware, and documentation. Three factors invoke adaptive maintenance: internal business needs, external competition, and external requirements.

Adaptive maintenance should be conducted using a top-down approach. Design begins at the system and data level where the major activities are:

- Review change request.
- Revise system design. Maintainers review data flow diagrams and system process explosions to identify affected data bases and processes. Changes are then designed.
- Revise data design. Maintainers access the data dictionary for data descriptions and record layouts. Needed changes are designed.
- Conduct design walk-throughs (human testing).
- Update documentation, and store software products in the configuration management system and the updated change request in the change request tracking system.

Next changes are designed at the program and module levels. The major activities are:

- Revise program design. Maintainers analyze data flow diagrams, structure or hierarchy charts, and written documentation to determine where to add, change, or delete functions.
- Revise module design. The structure or hierarchy charts and the specifications, written in a program design language or pseudocode, are analyzed for changes which are then implemented.
- Conduct design and code walk-throughs (human testing).
- Make revisions, and store software products in the configuration management system and change requests in the change management system.

The critical success factors that this chapter addressed are:

- Controlling changes and software products through change management and configuration management systems.
- Use of structured design and coding principles.
- Using incremental testing throughout the software maintenance process to improve the quality of the delivered product (specifically human testing—walk-throughs and inspections—to improve software quality).

This chapter described how to design enhancements at the system, data, program, and module levels. The next chapter describes how to cut the costs of corrective and adaptive maintenance by using perfective maintenance.

DISCUSSION QUESTIONS

1. What are the causes of adaptive maintenance problems?

2. What are the consequences of these problems?

3. If the maintainer had skipped the system design phase and just started looking at where to hook the inquiry system into the existing code, what sort of problems might have occurred during implementation of the change?

4. Which of the processes, programs, and modules would have been impacted if the designers had tried to integrate the rejected system design into the existing system?

CHAPTER

7

Perfective Maintenance

Why should you improve software that works? Wouldn't that waste time and money? These are questions maintainers often ask when a program works, but the quality could be improved. When software quality improves, costs shrink, programs become more maintainable, and users' satisfaction leaps. This chapter describes a technique for identifying software that needs quality improvements. After reading this chapter, you should be able to:

- Recognize the benefits of quality improvements.
- Develop a Pareto analysis.
- Use a Pareto analysis to identify perfective maintenance candidates.

In Chapter 5 it was stated that maintenance could be thought of as taking two steps forward and one step back. Therefore any method that *eliminates* or *reduces* the impact of changes can have a significant payoff in maintenance costs.

Perfective maintenance is such a method. Perfective maintenance includes all efforts to polish or refine the quality of the software or documentation.

The following examples illustrate the range of activities that are included under the perfective maintenance classification: reengineering, rewriting, and upgrading documentation. Restructuring poorly written code makes it easier to maintain. A detailed example will be shown in Chapter 8. Following restructuring, the code's *maintainability* and *flexibility* are improved, reducing the cost of corrective and adaptive maintenance.

It's common for software defects to cluster in a few programs or modules. An intensive inspection and correction of potential defects in these modules is perfective maintenance. It improves the system's *reliability* and reduces the cost of corrective maintenance.

Rewriting (in assembler language) or restructuring the most extensively used routine in the system (as identified by execution monitors) to maximize its *efficiency* is also perfective maintenance. Rewriting in assembler language, however, can reduce the software's *portability* and *maintainability*.

Upgrading documentation to a standard format and style will improve its *consistency, readability,* and *maintainability*.

Quality improvements can be as extensive as a complete redesign and rewrite of a program using structured design techniques, or be confined to one line of code. The size of the improvement is not particularly important; it *is* important that each improvement reduce the system's maintenance costs.

To illuminate this relatively unknown subject, this chapter:

- Presents typical problems found in a software maintenance environment when perfective maintenance is not used.
- Describes the features and benefits of perfective maintenance.
- Describes Pareto analysis—a process for selecting perfective maintenance candidates.

Figure 7.1 shows how perfective maintenance functions and how it fits into overall software maintenance process. Perfective maintenance consists of two processes:

1. Identifying candidates (before a system release is planned).
2. Correcting identified quality problems to maximize the benefits.

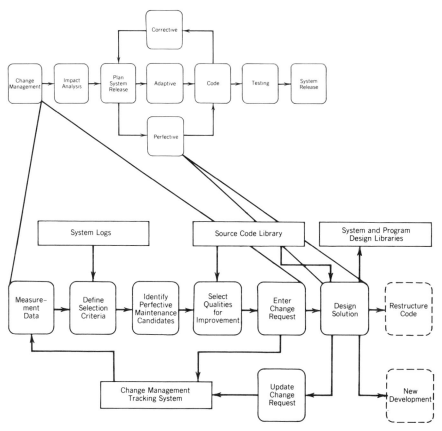

Figure 7.1 Perfective maintenance data flow

In the first step:

• Maintainers or quality assurance personnel define the criteria from which perfective maintenance candidates are to be chosen. This normally depends on available data and location of maintenance "hot spots."

• Then a Pareto analysis is conducted to identify perfective maintenance candidates.

• The result of the Pareto analysis is used to determine what quality improvements ought to be made. These can be improvements in maintainability, reliability, efficiency, or a variety of other qualities covered later in this module.

- A change request is then entered in the change management system to track the perfective maintenance work.

In the second step the problem-solving process discussed in Chapter 5 is used to improve the quality. In summary, this process:

- Defines the quality problem.
- Develops and tests a hypothesis.
- Resolves the problem.
- Updates the system design, program design, and change request.
- Restructures or rewrites the code or documentation to meet quality goals.

1. PERFECTIVE MAINTENANCE

As previously stated, perfective maintenance includes all efforts to improve the quality of software or documentation. It does not correct defects or change what the system does. Perfective maintenance focuses on improving expensive-to-maintain software.

Existing systems are profitable systems, but improper repairs can destroy the system's structure and hasten the system's entropy. Often, as systems are enhanced and repaired, more time is spent on repairing defects injected by previous changes. Eventually, as repairs become excessive, the system will cease to tolerate changes and will need to be replaced. Because replacement is an expensive process, every effort must be made to slow the decay of system software. That is the aim of perfective maintenance: to delay the day of unfixable obsolescence.

When consistently implemented, perfective maintenance can provide the following benefits:

- *Improved Maintainer Skill.* With practice, maintainers develop skills in improving program quality that can be used throughout their careers to minimize maintenance costs and to develop new systems that maximize maintainability.
- *Reduced Exposure to Risk.* Higher quality programs reduce the risks of schedule and budget overruns and program failures.
- *Reduced Maintenance Costs.* By improving the 20% of the programs that consume 80% of the costs or resources, maintenance costs can be measurably reduced.

- *More Time for Enhancements and New Development.* Perfective maintenance can reduce the number of hours spent fixing defects or making an enhancement. This newly available time can be channeled into implementing other enhancements and doing new development work.

- *Enhanced System Maintainability.* With structure, modularity, and comprehensive tolerance of software faults, emergency corrective maintenance can be whipped. Thus maintainers encounter fewer overtime hours and midnight calls, caused by hard-to-maintain systems.

2. SELECTING PERFECTIVE MAINTENANCE CANDIDATES

This section describes the *criteria* used to select perfective maintenance candidates and the *data* needed to identify those candidates. It also describes a "Pareto analysis" technique that *identifies* perfective maintenance candidates.

Many maintainers seem to know intuitively which programs and modules need perfective maintenance. Intuition, however, can be inaccurate, and ideas not supported by documentation are hard to sell. To obtain management and client support for perfective maintenance, it is important to document a case for quality improvement.

The procedure for documenting a perfective maintenance case consists of:

- Defining selection criteria
- Gathering related data
- Analyzing the data
- Implementing a solution
- Reviewing the benefits and results derived

As a first step, maintainers define the selection criteria for choosing perfective maintenance candidates—for example, most failures, most defects, and highest frequency of enhancement. Defining selection criteria focuses your attention on key problem areas and the data needed to document those problems.

These data vary by organization, but their purpose is always the same: to identify the best perfective maintenance candidates. Often these are programs that perform critical functions or require the most resources to maintain.

For example (Brooks 1975):

- In IBM's OS/360, 4% of the system modules contained 38% of the defects.
- In IBM's IMS/360, 31 modules out of 425 (8%) contained 57% of the errors.

Focusing on these modules would maximize the benefits of preventive maintenance.

As you might guess, Pareto analysis is a bean-counting approach. For it to work, you have to define ways to separate the beans (selection criteria). Some examples of selection criteria are:

- *Defect Type*. A defect is any failure to meet requirements—for example, programs with the most logic, computational, interface, or data manipulation errors (see Chapter 5 for a list of defects). Another way to classify defects is by severity code.
- *Defect Costs*. The costs of repairing defects—dollars, time, or equipment usage.
- *Symptom*. A symptom is an observable result of a defect—for example, a rounding defect where the reported total is off by one cent.
- *Cause*. A cause is a proven reason for the existence of a defect—for example, storing the results of a multiplication in a field that is too small (i.e., storing the results of $10 \star 10$ in a field two digits in length).
- *Failure Rate*. The number or frequency of failures can signal quality problems. This is also referred to as the mean time between failures (MTBF).
- *Failure Type*. Some examples are dividing by zero and incorrect logic.
- *Field Performance*. Some examples are slow response time, CPU hog, and core hog.
- *Enhancement Costs*. An example is total or average cost (in days, dollars, or CPU) per enhancement.
- *Enhancement Rate*. This rate is based on the number of changes requested per year.

Having defined and chosen one or more of these selection criteria, certain reliable sources of data can be used to identify or document these problems. Reliable sources of data are:

- Change request data base
- Historical change request logs
- Configuration management system histories
- Operating system logs
- Time-reporting/project management systems

A change request data base can contain most of the data needed to identify perfective maintenance candidates. If the change request contains the minimum contents discussed in Chapter 2, the following data would be available for each change:

- Systems affected
- Programs affected
- Modules affected
- Documents affected
- Estimated and actual time worked
- Type of change (i.e., corrective, adaptive, or perfective)
- Severity code

Historical data from the change request data base or the configuration management system is best used to identify high cost programs. After all, the more changes a system, program, or module receives, the more it needs to be highly maintainable and flexible.

Operating system logs can be examined to identify programs that fail most often, the major reasons for program failure (i.e., failure code), the mean time between failures, and the mean time to make repairs. Reliability improvements should be made to those programs that fall in the top 20% of these categories.

Operating system logs can also highlight which programs use the most computer resources, such as memory, tape drives, disk drives, and other peripheral devices. These data can be used to select programs for efficiency improvements.

The time-reporting or project management system can be used to identify time worked by program, module, task, or any other factor by which time is recorded. Some of the key variances to look for are:

- Overtime worked by system, program, and module.
- Total time worked by system, program, and module.

- Time spent on adaptive, corrective, or perfective maintenance.

- Overtime costs for corrective maintenance.

Now that you know what data to collect and where to find it, you need a technique to analyze and interpret the data. Pareto analysis is such a technique.

3. THE PARETO ANALYSIS

The Pareto analysis presented in this section seeks to identify the 20% of the programs that consume 80% of the budget and personnel resources (Juran 1979). This analysis is also known as the 80/20 rule; it is based on the principle of the *vital few* and the *trivial many*. In other words, the bulk of all programs (the trivial many) accounts for very little of the total effect (cost).

A Pareto analysis frequently takes the form of a matrix. Systems, programs, or modules are listed down the left side. Defects, failure types, time worked, or any other meaningful measurement data are listed along the top.

Once the matrix is constructed, it is filled in and analyzed. Candidates in the top 20% of the selection criteria should be selected for perfective maintenance.

Three Pareto matrices follow. The first matrix shows how *programs* are selected for perfective maintenance by using failures, defects, enhancements, and time worked as the selection criteria.

The second and third matrices show how further analysis can determine which *modules* to select for perfective maintenance.

Based on the Pareto analysis matrix that follows programs A and B should be selected for perfective maintenance:

- Program A to reduce the time spent on enhancing that module.

- Program B to reduce the high density of failures and defects.

PARETO ANALYSIS MATRIX: PROGRAM LEVEL

Programs	Failures	Defects	Enhancements	Time Worked
Program A	1	3	**15**	**20**
Program B	**10**	**17**	2	**15**
Program C	0	1	1	2
System XYZ	11	21	18	37

Further analysis, indicates that the following modules from programs *A* and *B* should be selected for perfective maintenance.

- Module 1 in program *A* to reduce the time spent on enhancing that module.
- Module 2 in program *B* to reduce the high density of failures and defects.

Any investment in the other programs and modules would be of negligible benefit.

PARETO ANALYSIS MATRIX: MODULE LEVEL
Program *A*

Module	Failures	Defects	Enhancements	Time Worked
Module 1	1	0	**12**	**15**
Module 2	0	3	2	3
Module 3	0	0	1	2
Totals	1	3	15	20

PARETO ANALYSIS MATRIX: MODULE LEVEL
Program *B*

Module	Failures	Defects	Enhancements	Time Worked
Module 1	1	1	1	2
Module 2	**9**	**15**	1	**12**
Module 3	0	1	0	1
Totals	10	17	2	15

Once candidates have been selected, maintainers must choose the qualities to improve and a solution for improving them.

4. QUALITY IMPROVEMENTS

Having identified the perfective maintenance candidates, the specific qualities to improve and a solution to achieve them can be selected. This section describes those activities.

Some widely accepted quality factors and their attributes are:

- Maintainability:

    Can you fix it?

    Does it take little effort to fix it, or modify the defect?

    Is it indented in a standard way?

    Is it well commented with prologue and decision points?

    Are the modules simple?

- Flexibility:

    Can you enhance it?

    Is the program free of "spaghetti" code (i.e., GOTOs)?

    Are there copy libraries for data definitions?

- Reliability:

    Will it run and produce the correct results everytime?

- Reusability:

    Can the system, program, or module be used in other applications
    to reduce development costs?

- Usability:

    Can the user/customer learn and use the system easily?

    Can operations run it?

- Efficiency:

    Does it run on your hardware as quickly as possible?

- Testability:

    Can you test it?

- Integrity:

    Is the application and its data secure from outside intrusion?

- Portability:

    Can the system easily move from one hardware and operating
    system environment to another?

- Interoperability:

    Can it interface easily with other systems?

- Correctness:

    Is the application and its data complete, accurate, and consistent?

Figure 7.2 shows the relationship between the selection criteria, discussed earlier, and the list of qualities just reviewed.

SELECTION CRITERIA

QUALITY	Defect Type	Symptom	Cause	Defect Costs	Failure Rate	Failure Type	Field Performance	Enhancement Costs	Enhancement Rate
Maintainability				•	•		•		
Flexibility							•	•	•
Reliability	•	•	•		•	•	•		
Reusability				•				•	
Usability							•		
Efficiency							•		
Testability	•	•	•	•	•	•			
Integrity	•					•			
Portability							•	•	
Interoperability							•	•	
Correctness	•					•			

Figure 7.2   Quality selection criteria

To interpret the matrix, locate the selection criteria on the top axis and read down the column, or read across for each quality. Each dot indicates a relationship between the selection criteria and the quality.

For example, if the selection criteria is *defect type,* the qualities to improve would be reliability, testability, and integrity. Conversely, if you wanted to improve maintainability, you would look at defect costs, failure rate, and field performance.

Not all quality improvements can coexist. Therefore you should understand the relationship between quality factors. Figure 7.3 shows the relationships among qualities. To read the diagram, locate the desired quality in the left column. Then read across the matrix to identify relationships with other qualities. In Figure 7.3:

- An unfilled dot indicates a high degree of commonality (i.e., maintainability and reliability).

- A filled dot indicates an adversarial relationship (note that efficiency is directly opposed to all other qualities).

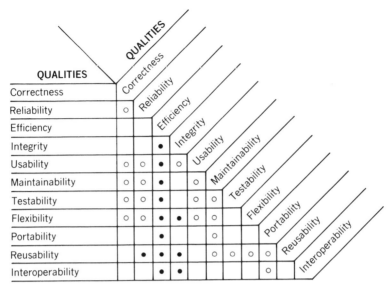

Figure 7.3 Quality relationships

- A blank cell indicates that no relationship exists between the qualities or that the relationship is application dependent.

The final perfective maintenance activity is to apply the problem-solving process described in Chapter 5 and to select a solution for achieving the desired improvements.

The major alternatives for correcting quality problems are: a complete redesign and rewrite, complete restructuring, partial restructuring, or system retirement and redevelopment. The guidelines for implementing each one are as follows:

- *Complete redesign and rewrite* (using structured design and programming techniques). Use this approach when:

  More than 20% of the program must be changed (e.g., the functionality of the program is radically changed by the user's requests).

  Program is being upgraded to a new technology (e.g., from sequential files to a data base).

  Do not use this approach when the design and function of the existing program are not known. Rewrites will fail to include all of the existing functionality, causing extensive corrective and adaptive maintenance.

- *Complete restructuring or overhaul of the existing code.* Use this technique on highly maintenance-prone programs. Choose a time when the program has minimal changes during a release. It will be easier to ensure that restructuring does not comprise its functionality.

- *Partial restructuring integrated with adaptive maintenance.* This approach provides an orderly improvement of the program with each system release. It stems from the Kernighan and Plauger axiom in *The Elements of Programming Style:* "Don't patch bad code—rewrite it," or in this case restructure it.

  Maintainers can select modules for partial restructuring based on changes required within the module. In fact maintainers can and should restructure every piece of code they enter when making a change (i.e., a COBOL paragraph, a FORTRAN subroutine, or a PL/I function).

- *Retirement of the system and complete redevelopment.* Retirement is the best solution when moving to a new technology (e.g., from sequential files to a data base) or when the costs of maintaining the software *and* hardware exceed the cost of redevelopment.

5. SUMMARY

Perfective maintenance is a two-step process: selecting candidates and improving the qualities selected. The key perfective maintenance activities are:

- Defining selection criteria
- Gathering related data
- Analyzing the data
- Implementing a solution

Perfective maintenance includes all efforts to improve the quality of software or documentation. Perfective maintenance focuses on improving only the most expensive-to-maintain programs.

When consistently implemented, perfective maintenance can *reduce* risks and maintenance costs and *increase* development time, system maintainability, maintainers' skills, and user satisfaction.

A Pareto analysis compares systems, programs, or modules with selected criteria to determine which ones consume the majority of resources. This analysis is used to determine what work to do, in what order, and for what reason.

A problem-solving process selects a means for achieving the improvements. The solution may be a complete redesign and rewrite, a complete or partial restructuring, or a retirement of the system and new development.

This chapter addressed one of the key critical success factors—gathering quality assurance data and using the data to refine software development and maintenance practices.

This chapter described the concept of perfective maintenance and how to develop a Pareto analysis matrix to select perfective maintenance candidates. It also described the relationship between selection criteria and qualities, and the relationships among qualities. The next chapter describes how to restructure code to achieve the promises of perfective maintenance.

DISCUSSION QUESTIONS

1. What are some common justifications for not doing perfective maintenance?

2. Why should you fix something that isn't broken? What are some reasons for performing perfective maintenance?

3. What could you do to show management and clients the value of making quality improvements?

CHAPTER

8

===

Reengineering
Source Code

This code is garbage . . . I want to rewrite it.

We don't have the time for you to spend a month rewriting a program that
already works!

I can't figure out how this code works. It's complex, difficult to read, uses
cryptic data names, has inadequate comments, and doesn't follow standards.
Just look at this statement, BRANCH TO ABILENE. What do you suppose
that means?

If this scenario sounds familiar to you, read on. Unstructured code is
difficult to understand and change. Often it is hard to decipher what the
code is supposed to do, how it's done, and how it represents the module or
program design. Most of the time there is no one from the original development team to ask for advice. Unstructured code is one of the major
reasons maintainers must spend so much time on maintenance work and
precious little time on development work.

But there *is* a method to reengineer code. It consists of two processes:
restructuring and redesign. It can help you correct quality problems and
pare maintenance costs down indefinitely.

We've all been confronted with a maintenance change where the underlying software resembled spaghetti rather than code, right? If the project was small, you might have been able to guess where to make the change, but if the project was large, it seemed impossible. Spaghetti code can be managed whether the project is small or large *if* you reengineer the code.

The purpose of this chapter is to demonstrate that messy code can be reengineered for future maintainability. After completing this chapter, you should be able to:

- Reengineer program code.
- Evaluate code changes for logic and quality problems.

This chapter will:

- Present typical problems maintainers face with unstructured code.
- Describe the purpose and benefits of reengineering code.
- Present examples of code problems and techniques for reengineering them.
- Present guidelines for producing well-structured code.
- Describe tools for reengineering code.

This chapter will not tell you how to fix code defects or make enhancements. There are too many different methods, situations, languages, applications, and so on. Besides, I assume that if you can find a problem, you can fix it. If you can design structured enhancements, you can implement them. But you may not know how to reengineer existing code to clarify its function and simplify changing it.

Figure 8.1 shows where the coding process fits into the maintenance process. It illustrates the following:

- The data flow diagram shows the coding process and how it fits into the overall software maintenance process.
- The diagram in the upper left-hand corner shows that coding is conducted after changes have been designed and before testing and system release. (But you knew that didn't you?)
- Exploded coding diagram shows the process begins with a review of change requests and design documents:

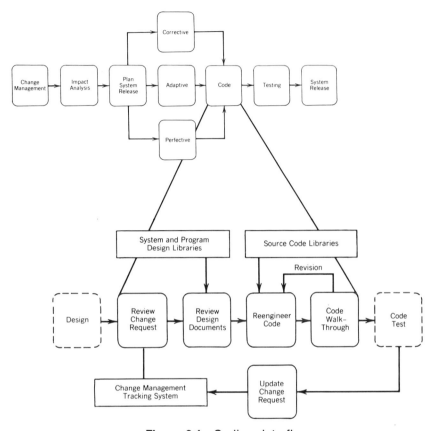

Figure 8.1 Coding data flow

Change requests are accessed through the change management
tracking system.

Design documentation is accessed through the system and program design libraries section of the configuration management
system.

- Having understood the requested quality changes, the code is reengineered using the process described in this chapter.

- A code walk-through identifies potential problems:

If the walk-through is successful, the code is tested.

If the walk-through is unsuccessful, the code is revised.

- Finally, the change request is updated and stored in change management tracking system.

1. RESTRUCTURING CODE

Chapter 7 described how to select qualities to improve in perfective maintenance candidates. This reading will describe how to improve those qualities. More specifically, this reading describes the purpose and benefits of restructuring source code. It then describes frequent code problems and approaches for correcting these problems.

The purpose of restructuring code is to improve its quality. The qualities to improve may include one or more of the following:

- Maintainability
- Flexibility
- Reliability
- Reusability
- Usability
- Efficiency
- Testability
- Integrity
- Portability
- Interoperability
- Correctness

To improve the code's quality, use structured coding techniques to reduce the code's complexity and improve its structure.

Some of the benefits of using structured coding practices are:

- It takes maintainers less time to fix structured code by as much as a factor of four (Capers Jones 1985).
- It takes less time to implement enhancements, leaving more time for new development.
- More value can be provided to the company in less time. Maintainers achieve higher satisfaction from accomplishing more and better work.
- Structured code does not fail as often, reducing costly downtime and rework.
- It's easier to learn the code in structured programs. (Learning the code is the first step in correcting or enhancing program code.)

For each quality there are typically a number of code problems that require restructuring. The following paragraphs will describe some code problems that affect maintainability, flexibility, reusability, reliability, and efficiency. They also present examples of how code can be restructured to improve these qualities.

2. MAINTAINABILITY AND FLEXIBILITY

There are many reasons why code can be difficult to maintain or enhance. Some of the key ones are:

- Poor readability
- Complex decision logic
- Use of GOTOs
- Size in lines of code

To improve maintainability or flexibility, you must first understand these typical problems.

2.1. Readability

Readability is characterized by clear, concise code that is immediately understandable. The following example labeled "unstructured" illustrates hard-to-read code.

Unstructured:

```
LABEL_1:
READ A RECORD;
IF END_OF_FILE GOTO LABEL3; ENDIF
IF FIELD_1 NOT = '1' AND FIELD_1 NOT = '2' GOTO
LABEL_2; ENDIF
IF FIELD_1 NOT = '3' AND FIELD_1 NOT = '4' GOTO
LABEL_2; ENDIF
OUT_FIELD_1 = FIELD_1;
LABEL_2:
IF NOT END_OF_FILE GOTO LABEL_1; ENDIF
LABEL_3:
```

The following "structured" example illustrates how the code can be restructured to improve readability. Notice, that in the restructured example there is only one statement per line and that the code is indented under IF, CASE, and LOOP statements. Structuring engines and code beautifiers can be used to automate the work.

Structured:

```
CHAR FIELD_1_MINIMUM_VALUE = '1';
CHAR FIELD_1_MAXIMUM_VALUE = '4';

READ A RECORD;              /* READ THE FIRST RECORD */

DOUNTIL ( END_OF_FILE )  /* READ ALL RECORDS */

  IF FIELD_1 >= FIELD_1_MINIMUM_VALUE AND
     FIELD_1 <= FIELD_1_MAXIMUM_VALUE

      OUT_FIELD_1 = FIELD_1;

  ELSE

      ;  /* FALL THROUGH TO THE NEXT STATEMENT */

  ENDIF

  READ A RECORD;  /* READ NEXT RECORD */

ENDDO
```

2.2. Complex Decision Logic

Decisions (IF_ELSE, CASE, DOUNTIL, and DOWHILE) are simple logical constructs. It's only when they are coupled together in unusual ways that they become complex and difficult to maintain.

Most research indicates that the nesting level (number of decisions nested inside of other decisions) should not exceed three for maximum clarity and understanding of the code (Baker 1981). Other studies indicate that the number of decisions in a module/unit of code should not exceed 10 for maximum maintainability (McCabe 1976).

In the following example, the left side illustrates problems involving complex decision logic; the right side shows how the code can be restructured to reduce complexity.

Example 1:

```
IF A = B THEN                    IF A = B OR C = D THEN
   PROCESS(A,B,C,D)                 PROCESS (A,B,C,D)
ELSE IF C = D THEN               ELSE
   PROCESS(A,B,C,D)                 EXCEPTION PROCESSING
ELSE
   EXCEPTION PROCESSING
```

Example 2:

```
IF A = B THEN                    IF A = B AND C = D THEN
   IF C = D THEN                    PROCESS (A,B,C,D)
      PROCESS(A,B,C,D)          ELSE
ELSE                                EXCEPTION PROCESSING
   EXCEPTION PROCESSING          ENDIF
ENDIF
```

Notice, that a decision and a call to PROCESS were removed from the example on the right without changing the function of the code. Notice that the nesting level is reduced to one in the restructured example. Both changes reduced decision complexity.

2.3. NOT Logic

If something is *not* white, it is *not* necessarily black. It could be green or yellow, right? NOT logic is a particularly nasty element of complex decision logic. NOT logic, by its negative statement, omits more than it tells, which is why programmers have such a hard time understanding them. This is especially true when they are coupled together with boolean ANDs and ORs.

In the following example the left side illustrates a problem with NOT logic; the right side shows how the code can be restructured to eliminate NOT logic:

```
IF A NOT = B THEN                IF A = B THEN
   EXCEPTION PROCESSING             /* FALL THROUGH */
ENDIF                            ELSE
                                    EXCEPTION PROCESSING
                                 ENDIF


IF A NOT = B AND                 IF A = B OR C = D THEN
C NOT = D THEN
   EXCEPTION PROCESSING             /* FALL THROUGH */
ENDIF                            ELSE
                                    EXCEPTION PROCESSING
                                 ENDIF
```

Notice, that reversing the NOT logic, in most cases, requires the addition of an ELSE part of the IF. This is the most structured, maintainable way of writing a decision. One of the most frequent logic errors is *missing logic*. This change will illuminate the default logic. Also notice that reversing the NOTs reverses the AND/OR test in the second example.

2.4. GOTOs

GOTOs can be a problem. They are about the only way to violate the structure of code. Some languages don't provide the facilities to loop easily, so the GOTO must be used, but used carefully. GOTOs should return to their point of origin, because that's how loops work. They should only branch downward in the structure of the code, not up.

In the following example the left side has multiple GOTOs, and the right side shows how the code was restructured to eliminate them:

```
READ-LOOP                   READ A RECORD
   READ A RECORD            WHILE MORE RECORDS
   IF END OF FILE              PROCESS RECORD
      GO TO READ-EXIT         READ A RECORD
   PROCESS RECORD           END WHILE
   GO TO READ-LOOP
READ-EXIT
```

Notice that the structured example replaced an IF and a GOTO with a single WHILE statement. The addition of the first READ eliminated the need for the other GOTO. READs don't violate structure; GOTOs do. Automated restructuring engines for many languages can help accomplish this work.

2.5. Size/Redundant Code

Code modules larger than 100 executable lines can often contain as much as 30% redundant code (Arthur 1985). Redundant, or duplicate, code causes many maintenance problems because a change to one copy of the code does not change all of the embedded versions. Once you've changed 15 identical pieces of code over the period of several days of testing, you begin to get the idea. Redundant code can be eliminated by restructuring the code to use a single copy. The code can remain in-line or, if it's large enough, be moved to a separate module that is called where needed. A single routine to edit social security numbers should be much easier to maintain than hundreds of such routines spread throughout a payroll system.

In the following example the left side shows two chunks of redundant code; the right side shows how the code can be restructured to eliminate the redundancy.

Again, notice that one decision is eliminated and two assignment and addition statements are removed. The *size* of this chunk of code was reduced from six executable lines of code (ELOC) to only three, reducing maintenance costs by one half.

```
IF A = B THEN                    IF A = B OR C = D THEN
   E = A + B                        E = A + B
   F = C + D                        F = C + D
ELSE IF C = D THEN               ELSE
   E = A + B                        EXCEPTION PROCESSING
   F = C + D                     ENDIF
ELSE
   EXCEPTION PROCESSING
ENDIF
```

3. REUSABILITY

Many modules contain two or more unique functions which, if separated from the main body of code, could be reused with other programs. For

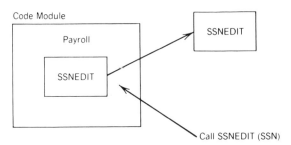

Figure 8.2 Breaking out reusable modules

example, if a module contained two functions, a payroll function and a social security edit function, it could be separated so that the social security edit function could be used with any other function (see Figure 8.2). As it is, the social security edit function is not reusable.

As you can see, separating functions into their own modules allows each function to be reused with other modules. It also breaks the module into smaller units of code that are easier to maintain (under 100 ELOC and 10 decisions). Maintenance costs will shrink to a fraction of their previous levels because each module will be less complex. Reengineering code into separate functions often takes more time than restructuring within the existing module; but redesign of expensive-to-maintain modules to maximize reuse will maximize return on investment.

In the following example the left side shows a simple example of duplicate code. Notice that to change the value of E or F the change would have to be written in two places, increasing maintenance costs and the possibility of an error. The right side shows how the code was restructured for reusability. Notice that the function, PROCESS, can be reused as needed.

```
IF A = B THEN          IF A = B THEN
    E = A + B              PROCESS(A,B,C,D,E,F)
    F = C + D          ELSE
ENDIF                      EXCEPTION PROCESSING
    .                  ENDIF
    .                      .
    .                      .
IF C = D THEN              .
    E = A + B          IF C = D THEN
    F = C + D              PROCESS(A,B,C,D,E,F)
ENDIF                  ELSE
```

```
              EXCEPTION PROCESSING
          ENDIF
          PROCESS(A,B,C,D,E,F)
              E = A + B
              F = C + D
          END PROCESS
```

Although this example may seem trivial, using the same technique, I reduced the size of one COBOL program from 1500 to 700 executable statements. In another I reduced it from 2000 to one module of 1000 ELOC and another of 250. The second module was called four times, using different data. You can do the same.

4. RELIABILITY

Unreliable programs fail frequently, or produce incorrect data. Most of the examples and factors shown in this section also affect the quality *correctness*.

4.1. Correctness

The correctness of data, especially when used in arithmetic statements, affects reliability. The most common example in the IBM world involves "packing" a numeric field filled with blanks and then trying to use the packed field in an arithmetic operation giving the dreaded OC7 abend.

Another example involves dividing by zero, without testing the divisor for zeros. The following code shows two different ways of testing for a zero divisor:

```
IF D = 0 THEN                    A = C / D
    EXCEPTION PROCESSING             ON OVERFLOW
ELSE                                     EXCEPTION PROCESSING
    A = C / D
```

Unreliable programs, however, will contain only the single statement; A = C/D. Data should always be examined before use. This technique is known as *mutual suspicion*.

The following example shows how incorrectly defined overlays of data structures can cause data errors and program failures. In the example on the left the elements under ITEM-2 (NEW-DATE and B) incorrectly redefine the first two fields. The example on the right shows how to correct the error:

```
GROUP-ITEM                      GROUP-ITEM
  CHAR A                          CHAR A
  INT DATE                        INT DATE
  ITEM-2 REDEFINES GROUP-ITEM     ITEM-2 REDEFINES ...
  INT NEW-DATE                    CHAR B
  CHAR B                          INT NEW-DATE
```

4.2. Logic

Logic problems fall into several categories:

- Missing logic—ELSE path for each IF; DEFAULTS for each CASE.
- Incorrect action following a decision—taking the wrong action following an IF or CASE. Sometimes the actions are reversed—the IF action should follow the ELSE and the ELSE action should follow the IF.
- Incorrect number of iterations in a DOWHILE or DOUNTIL.

In the next example the left side illustrates a logic problem; the right shows the corrected code. Notice that the left loop will only execute 89 times, not 90.

```
/* Calculate sine of angles from 1–90 degrees */
angle = 1                       angle = 1
DOWHILE( angle < 90 )           DOWHILE ( angle <= 90 )
  PRINT(SINE(angle))              PRINT(SINE(angle))
  angle = angle + 1               angle = angle + 1
ENDWHILE                        ENDWHILE
```

Every language has other specific reliability problems. These are but a few of the common ones encountered in any language or application. The remaining major quality problem rears its ugly head in the efficiency of real time and transaction-driven systems.

5. EFFICIENCY

As shown in Chapter 7, efficiency works in opposition to all of the other quality goals. Efficient code is typically not as maintainable, flexible, or reliable as code targeted at these goals. Efficient code takes the least amount of time to execute a program correctly. Software is usually inefficient because of the way the data was designed or the code was written. Reengineering can correct these problems.

If a single subroutine consumes the majority of the CPU resources for a given program, then its algorithm should be examined and tuned up to improve its processing. Performing this type of maintenance on all subroutines would be a waste of time unless there is a contractual requirement for unusual response time.

The following lists various ways to improve efficiency:

- Move all code that need only be executed once, outside of loops (usually the code that initializes variables).

- Terminate loops early whenever possible (i.e., once a match has been found in a table—don't loop through the rest of the table).

- Put the most commonly matched values at the front of the table to minimize most linear search times.

- Test to see if the new value matches the last value looked up to eliminate the need for a search. This only works if repeats are common.

- Calculate common subexpressions only once. For example:

```
A = B + C       A = B + C
D = B + C       D = A
```

- Find more efficient algorithms (i.e., a quick sorting algorithm instead of a bubble sort, or a binary search instead of a sequential one).

- Input/output is the most time-consuming activity in most business programs. Design the data to minimize access wherever possible.

- Put numeric data in the most efficient format until such data need to be displayed. Binary or packed numbers can be operated on many times faster than display numerics.

- Align all of the program's data as well as possible to minimize unnecessary conversion and moves of the data. Character fields, of a certain size, may need to be double-word aligned, whereas shorter fields may be word or half-word aligned. Numeric fields should be properly aligned and of equal lengths when used in calculations (otherwise, the compiler has to convert them to the same length to perform arithmetic operations).

- Use optimizing compilers whenever possible. They often reduce execution time by 25%.
- Use an analyzer to determine where to concentrate efficiency work in a given program or system.

6. RESTRUCTURING CODE: AN EXAMPLE

Maintainers often feel that messy code cannot be rejuvenated. To minimize the frustration of trying to straighten out code, use an iterative process of simplification to make the code more maintainable.

Also, to make code more maintainable, reduce the number of statements required to accomplish a function, as well as the complexity of the decision logic (eliminating GOTOS, NOTs, IFs) wherever possible.

An example is shown on the next few pages. It illustrates how spaghetti code can be transformed into an easily maintainable chunk of code by using an iterative process of simplification.

6.1. The Mess

In the mess of spaghetti code that we started with, notice how all the lines are crammed together and left justified:

```
LABEL_1:
READ A RECORD;
IF END_OF_FILE GOTO LABEL3; ENDIF
IF FIELD_1 NOT = '1' AND FIELD_1 NOT = '2' GOTO
LABEL_2; ENDIF
IF FIELD_1 NOT = '3' AND FIELD_1 NOT = '4' GOTO
LABEL_2; ENDIF
OUT_FIELD_1 = FIELD_1;
WRITE NEW_RECORD
LABEL_2:
IF NOT END_OF_FILE GOTO LABEL_1; ENDIF
LABEL_3:
```

6.2. The First Pass

The first pass is to beautify, indent, and split up lines so that there is only one statement per line and the logic is clearer. The following example shows the code after this is done. Notice how much easier it is to read this chunk of code compared to it's original version.

```
LABEL_1:

  READ A RECORD;

  IF END_OF_FILE
    GOTO LABEL3;
  ENDIF

  IF FIELD_1 NOT = '1' AND FIELD_1 NOT = '2'
    GOTO LABEL_2;
  ENDIF

  IF FIELD_1 NOT = '3' AND FIELD_1 NOT = '4'
    GOTO LABEL_2;
  ENDIF

  OUT_FIELD_1 = FIELD_1;

  WRITE NEW_RECORD

LABEL_2:

  IF NOT END_OF_FILE
    GOTO LABEL_1;
  ENDIF

LABEL_3:
```

6.3. The Second Pass

Next the NOT logic is restructured to state things positively. Notice how the replacement of ANDs with ORs accomplishes this.

```
LABEL_1:

  READ A RECORD;

  IF END_OF_FILE
    GOTO LABEL3;
  ENDIF

  IF FIELD_1 = '1' OR FIELD_1 = '2'
    OUT_FIELD_1 = FIELD_1;
  ELSE
    GOTO LABEL_2;
  ENDIF

  IF FIELD_1 = '3' OR FIELD_1 = '4'
    OUT_FIELD_1 = FIELD_1;
  ELSE
    GOTO LABEL_2;
  ENDIF

  WRITE NEW_RECORD

LABEL_2:

  IF END_OF_FILE
    ;  /* FALL THROUGH TO THE NEXT LABEL*/
  ELSE
    GOTO LABEL_1;
  ENDIF

LABEL_3:
```

6.4. The Third Pass

Next the duplicate, or extraneous, code is eliminated. Notice how some of the GOTOs and IFs can be eliminated to make the code less complex.

```
LABEL_1:

  READ A RECORD;

  IF END_OF_FILE
    GOTO LABEL3;
  ENDIF

  IF FIELD_1 = '1' OR FIELD_1 = '2' OR
    FIELD_1 = '3' OR FIELD_1 = '4'
      OUT_FIELD_1 = FIELD_1;
  ELSE
    WRITE NEW_RECORD;
  ENDIF

  IF END_OF_FILE
    ;  /* FALL THROUGH TO THE NEXT LABEL */
  ELSE
    GOTO LABEL_1;  /* LOOP UNTIL ALL RECORDS ARE
    READ */
  ENDIF

LABEL_3:
```

6.5. The Fourth Pass

Next more powerful statements in the language are used to improve the
clarity of the algorithm. Notice how the looping statements (DOUNTIL)
and (ENDDO) replace the GOTOs. Also notice how comments are added
to clarify the algorithm.

```
READ A RECORD;  /* PRIME THE PUMP BY READING THE
                   FIRST RECORD */

DOUNTIL ( END_OF_FILE )  /* READ ALL OF THE RECORDS */

  IF FIELD_1 = '1' OR FIELD_1 = '2' OR
    FIELD_1 = '3' OR FIELD_1 = '4'
      OUT_FIELD_1 = FIELD_1;
```

```
    ELSE
      WRITE NEW_RECORD;
    ENDIF

    READ A RECORD;

  ENDDO
```

6.6. The Fifth Pass

Additional ways to clean up the logic, or algorithm, are implemented to make processing as clear as possible. This is accomplished by adding greater than ($>$) and less than ($<$) signs. Also an additional comment is included.

```
  READ A RECORD;   /* PRIME THE PUMP BY READING THE
                       FIRST RECORD */

  DOUNTIL ( END_OF_FILE )   /* READ ALL OF THE RECORDS
                               */

    IF FIELD_1 >= '1' AND FIELD_1 <= '4'
      OUT_FIELD_1 = FIELD_1;
    ELSE
      WRITE NEW_RECORD;
    ENDIF

    READ A RECORD; /* READ NEXT RECORD BEFORE UNTIL
                      TEST */

  ENDDO
```

6.7. The Final Pass

Finally, literals (like "1") are changed to meaningful names.

```
  CHAR FIELD_1_MINIMUM_VALUE = '1';
  CHAR FIELD_1_MAXIMUM_VALUE = '4';

  READ A RECORD; /* PRIME THE PUMP BY READING THE
                    FIRST RECORD */
```

```
DOUNTIL ( END_OF_FILE ) /* READ ALL OF THE RECORDS */

  IF FIELD_1 >= FIELD_1_MINIMUM_VALUE AND
    FIELD_1 <= FIELD_1_MAXIMUM_VALUE
      OUT_FIELD_1 = FIELD_1;
  ELSE
    WRITE NEW_RECORD;
  ENDIF

  READ A RECORD; /* READ NEXT RECORD BEFORE UNTIL
                     TEST */

ENDDO
```

The following chart shows how the previous changes reduced the number of statements and complexity of decision logic.

Notice that the size, in statements, has been cut in half; this will reduce maintenance costs by half. Decision complexity has been cut in half, and this can contribute to further reductions in maintenance effort. Complexity was also reduced by the removal of the NOTs and GOTOs. Since there are no GOTOs, there is no way to violate structure in this piece of code. The number of comments, describing the code, have increased to three and improved the code's readability.

Number of:	Old Code	New Code
Statements	11	6
Decisions	4	2
GOTOS	4	0
NOTS	5	0
Labels	3	0
Comments	0	3

7. REENGINEERING CODE: GUIDELINES

Restructuring code can be difficult even for the best programmers. To help with restructuring, this section will present guidelines on when and how to restructure code. It also provides a checklist to evaluate the work.

7.1. General Guidelines

Any code that is hard to understand should be restructured. This type of code may be messy, unclear, extraneous, or not concise.

It is best to reengineer code *one step at a time,* retesting between each revision. The reason for this is that the thought process for one restructuring step differs from another. When programmers try to do more than one process at a time, like removing NOTs and GOTOs, they often miss some of the code or restructure it incorrectly. Focusing on one step at a time will minimize human error and speed up debugging.

The best concept to adopt when restructuring code is to use structured programming techniques. This will help ensure the quality of the restructured code.

Use automated tools like code beautifiers, syntax checkers, code auditors, and quality analyzers to help do the work and to ensure the best implementation.

As reengineering work continues, develop or update the system documentation. This documentation includes:

- System design
- Program design
- Module design
- Test cases

7.2. Specific Reengineering Guidelines

Size

- Module size should be limited to a maximum of 100 executable lines of code to ensure functional strength. There are few exceptions (one is when the number of decisions is less than 10).
- Code should contain only one executable verb per line.
- Modularize by size and functional strength.

Decisions

- Keep decisions to a maximum of 10 decisions per module (McCabe, Structured Testing, IEEE Computer Society, 1983).

    This minimizes debugging time in development and corrective maintenance costs (Curtis, "Predicting performance on software maintenance tasks with the Halstead and McCabe metrics," *IEEE Trans. on Soft. Eng.,* 1979, v(5), pp. 95–104).

- Reverse NOT logic to state conditions positively.

Indenting

• Use indenting to show structure and grouping.

   Indent code under decision statements (IF, CASE, DOWHILE, DOUNTIL).

Nesting

• Avoid nesting decisions more than three levels deep.

• Use subroutines to break the decisions into more easily understand-able groups.

GOTOs

• Avoid or eliminate GOTOs, NOTs, and statements that alter the program's execution (i.e., the ALTER verb in COBOL).

   Use looping algorithms instead of GOTOs or ALTERs.

Functionality

• Use one function per module to maximize maintainability, flexibility, and reusability. This is known as *functional strength* (Myers 1976).

Data

• Use standard calling sequences.

   The module should be *data coupled,* which is to say that it should only receive or return *data* from its calling programs.

   It should not receive or send *flags* or *indicators* that affect its operation.

   It should not access or update *global* data.

• Use table-driven techniques wherever possible to minimize logic changes.

• Use arrays and tables to simplify processing and reduce complex decision logic (i.e., search a table instead of test for dozens of values).

• Design the data to minimize redundancy and maximize efficiency.

• Declare all variables and initialize them.

Reusable Code

• Create or reuse routines wherever possible.

   Use library functions (i.e., sine) and reusable functions (i.e., a social security number edit) to minimize maintenance costs.

Literals
- Avoid literals.

    Use meaningful data names for constants.

    Write clearly and concisely.

Fault Tolerance
- Anticipate and tolerate faults (bad input, division by zero, etc.).
- Don't let the program fail.

Naming
- Use meaningful data names and labels.

    For example, don't use BRANCH TO ALICE or ALICE = ANN/ APE or variations on these themes.
- Use a program/module name that is mnemonic but also contains a version identifier to simplify configuration management (i.e., PROG8701).
- Check that names are unique.
- Eliminate unused data names (i.e., names that could be used incorrectly by future maintainers).

Language
- Use high-level languages that support the five types of structured constructs:

    IF-ELSE

    CASE

    DOWHILE

    DOUNTIL

    Sequential ($+$, $*$, $=$, etc.)

- If possible, avoid assembler language and nonportable extensions to the language (all vendors add them to trap you in their hardware).

Comments
- Incorporate a prose description of the processing as part of the introductory comments.
- Use comments to explain what the code does *not* show clearly.

- Use comments to connect code to implementations of algorithms (especially complex, nonstandard algorithms).
- Add a block comment to the beginning of each unit of code that describes its name, purpose, limitations, inputs (and where they come from) outputs (where they go), algorithms used, assumptions, and references to documentation.
- Use comments to explain calls to external subroutines, complex decisions, and each logical group of code within the module (e.g., a loop that processes all data).
- Check comments for clarity and usefulness.

Number Versions

- Use number versions to control the configuration of the software and documentation. This is usually handled by the configuration management system.

Documentation

- Refer to the literature to document basic algorithms.
- Consistently follow documentation standards.

Using these guidelines, it's possible to develop a checklist to evaluate restructured and newly developed code.

8. EVALUATING REENGINEERED CODE

The checklist that follows can be used to evaluate reengineered code. It covers the code's structure, documentation, comments, data, interfaces, error handling, consistency, and completeness. This checklist was compiled by the National Bureau of Standards.

Following the general and specific reengineering guidelines presented in this reading can help make a seemingly difficult task easier and more accurate.

Reengineered Code Checklist

Structure

- Does the program exceed established size standards?
- Does the program have only one entrance and one exit?

- Does the processing flow from top to bottom?
- Does the number of decisions exceed established complexity standards?
- Does the number of functions exceed established standards?

Documentation/Comments

- Are there prologue comments that identify function, inputs and outputs, variables, author, modifications made, limitations, etc.?
- Are decisions commented?
- Are variables commented?
- Are branches commented?
- Is all machine language commented?
- Do comments do more than repeat the operation?
- Are consistent indentation and spacing used?

Data

- Are all variable names unique?
- Does each variable have only one unique name? What are its aliases?
- Are variables used in only one way?
- Are global variables used consistently with respect to units and type?
- Are all elements of an array/table functionally related?
- Are all variables initialized before use?
- Are all default variables described?
- Are arrays/tables/strings initialized before use?

Interfaces

- Are all calls to other programs commented?
- Are all arguments within *calls* parameters?
- Does the calling program maintain control?

Error Handling

- Are inputs *range tested?*
- Are possible conflicts or illegal combinations of inputs checked?
- Is there a check to determine if all necessary data are available prior to processing?
- Are loop and branch index parameters *range tested?*

- Are subscripts *range tested?*
- When an error condition occurs, is it passed to a calling module?
- Are the results of a computation checked before reporting or processing continues?
- Are all unusual termination conditions described?
- Are error messages descriptive and necessary actions explained?

Consistency/Completeness

- Does the code represent the design?
- Are all global variables defined?
- Are all called programs defined?
- Is all of the code reachable?
- Are all labels necessary?
- Are nonstandard language features avoided?
- Is self-modifying code avoided?

This seems like a lot to ask of a maintenance staff that is probably already in a time crunch, but they are questions worth asking and answering. Automated tools can often examine the code and answer them for you.

9. CODING TOOLS

Many of the tasks involved in *restructuring* code can be accomplished with the aid of code beautifiers and restructuring engines. This section describes the features, benefits, and limitations of these tools.

The benefits of using code beautifiers and restructuring engines are that they:

- Automate restructuring.
- Minimize clerical errors normally associated with restructuring.
- Can handle large, complex modules that would be difficult for a programmer to restructure.

9.1. Restructuring Engines

Restructuring engines are available for many languages. They automate part of the restructuring process. The features of restructuring engines are that they can:

- Replace GOTOs with loops.
- Move the code around to maximize efficiency.
- Restructure complex decision logic.
- Indent code and correct data-naming conventions.

The benefits gained from using these tools are that they can:

- Easily restructure spaghetti and GOTO-ladden code.
- More reliably restructure large modules than programmers can.

Some of the limitations of restructuring engines are:

- Restructuring engines only eliminate part of the reengineering job. They can't redesign programs, eliminate duplicate code, use better algorithms, or separate the functions into modular or reusable modules.
- Once the module is restructured, it still has to be tested and debugged
- The programmer has to relearn the restructured code. Manual restructuring ensures that the programmer understands the code when it's finished.
- They are not available for all languages (e.g., mainly SUPER-STRUCTURE, RECODER in COBOL).

9.2. Code Beautifiers

Code beautifiers improve the readability of any program or module. The features of code beautifiers are that they:

- Indent the code.
- Place one verb per line.

The benefits of using code beautifiers are simply improved readability and maintainability.

The only limitation of code beautifiers is that they may not meet local standards for indentation.

10. SUMMARY

Maintainers often resist reengineering code because the process or the code is too difficult to understand. Managers often resist it because they don't want to rewrite programs, just change them to meet deadlines.

The main purpose of reengineering code is to improve one or more of its qualities. Some of these qualities are maintainability, flexibility, reliability, and efficiency.

Some of the benefits of reengineering code are reduced maintenance costs and program failures. This can lead to increased user satisfaction and more time for new development.

To achieve these benefits, structured coding practices should be used to address code problems that involve maintainability, flexibility, reusability, reliability and efficiency.

Automated tools, like restructuring engines and code beautifiers can help restructure complex code. These tools automate restructuring, minimize clerical errors, and handle large, complex modules that would be difficult for programmers to restructure.

This chapter addressed the following critical success factors:

• Use of structured design and coding principles.

• Introduction and use of modern automated tools to improve quality and productivity.

This chapter demonstrated how to reengineer code. The next chapter describes how to test the revised (reengineered) software in an incremental fashion using both humans and machines.

DISCUSSION QUESTIONS

1. What problems do people have when rewriting or reengineering a code?

2. What were the causes of these problems?

3. What are the potential benefits of enhancing code?

4. Why is it important to reengineer code one step at a time?

CHAPTER

9

Software Testing

It's down to the wire. You weren't ready for unit test, so you skipped it and tested the whole program. Then you didn't have time for system testing and released the product anyway to meet an unreasonable deadline. After the release your client complains about its quick failure. Now, however, you have time to fix it, but work on the next release has to be delayed.

Sound familiar? Planning and conducting incremental testing can help you release products on time, without flaws, added overtime, or a contract penalty.

After reading this chapter, you should be able to:

- Describe the testing process.
- Describe human and computer testing.
- Describe the contents of a test plan.
- Recognize the features and benefits of various test tools.
- Describe the contents of a software test plan.

181

This chapter provides an overview of testing existing systems. It defines testing, explains the difference between testing in maintenance and development environments, and describes the concept of incremental testing, with its two components: human and computer testing.

1. TESTING

Testing is the process of executing a program with the intent of finding errors. A test that finds an error *is* a successful test (Myers 1979).

The objectives of testing are to:

- Ensure compliance with the original requirements and the approved changes.
- Ensure a quality product. Testing is a major component of a successful quality control plan.

Testing in a maintenance environment is similar to testing in a development environment. The principal differences are:

- Only changes need to be reviewed, not the entire product.
- Only new test cases that exercise the change need to be developed. They can then be added to the existing test bed.
- Only the existing test cases associated with changed products, along with any new test cases, will be needed to test the changes.
- Test results can be mechanically compared against previous test results to identify variations in the output caused by the changes. This comparison process is commonly known as regression testing.

2. MAINTENANCE TESTING

Testing may take up to 50% of the development budget (Brooks 1975) and a similar amount of the maintenance budget to ensure a high-quality product. Therefore it is essential to plan the testing process adequately.

Brook's (1975) Rule of Thumb for allocating maintenance work is:

- One-third planning and design
- One-sixth coding
- One-quarter component and early system test
- One-quarter system test with all components in hand

It is easier, however, to test the system incrementally, as designs, code, and programs are revised.

2.1. Incremental Testing

Test planning is based on the principle of incremental testing. Incremental testing integrates human and computer testing (Figure 9.1) to test the documentation and software in small chunks. Incremental testing breaks testing into a series of discrete tests that build on each other to ensure the system's reliability.

One advantage of incremental testing is that maintainers can begin testing early in the maintenance cycle and eliminate many defects in the requirements and design phases. By integrating the system in stages, a narrow set of interfaces are tested one at a time. This "build a little, test a little" philosophy is a way to maximize productivity and minimize risks associated with maintenance.

Other advantages of incremental testing are:

- Require less work, not more work:

    Incremental testing spreads the work over the maintenance process, rather than concentrate it at the end. This prevents reliability problems in the delivered product.

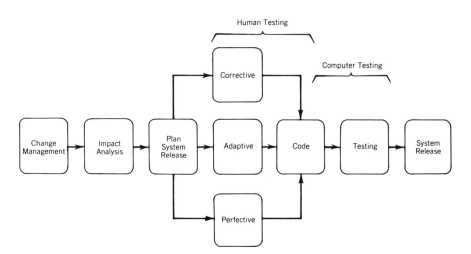

Figure 9.1 Incremental human and computer testing

- Programming errors are detected earlier:

    Defects found in requirements, design, and code are easier to isolate and correct than when found in integration or system test.

- Debugging is easier because the extent or domain of any problem is restricted:

    During design, only the system or program design are at fault and the *cause* of the defect is known.

    During unit test, only the revised module and the specific changes need to be examined.

    During integration test, with unit test complete, only the interfaces between modules and programs need to be examined.

    During system test, only the human-to-machine and program-to-program interfaces need to be examined.

- Testing is more thorough because modules are subjected to more testing exposure (once in code inspection, unit test, integration test, and system test).

- Resource scheduling is improved because of the opportunities for parallel activities:

    For example, each maintainer can unit test his/her own modules while everyone else codes and tests theirs.

    Once unit testing is complete for a program, integration test of that program can overlap other unit and integration tests.

    If design, code, and test are performed top-down, system testing can begin as soon as the first programs are ready, not at the last minute.

The data collected during impact analysis identify what must be tested at each level. This information is pulled together into a test plan, test procedures, and test cases.

2.2. Test Plan

Test plans should be based on an impact analysis, they describe how and when a system will be tested. Figure 9.2 shows how a system release, consisting of seven change requests, will affect a system's products. A test plan should identify the strategy for testing each component at each phase of the maintenance process. Some specific items to consider when developing a test plan are:

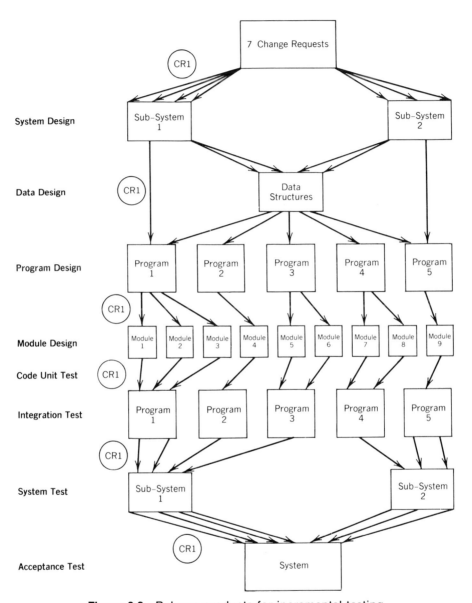

Figure 9.2 Release products for incremental testing

185

- Testing requirements/specifications
- List of programs, data bases, and documentation to be tested
- New test cases
- Required documentation of test case results
- Testing schedule and budget
- Approvals required at each stage of testing
- Test procedures

Using the ACE Co. example previously developed (Figure 9.3), a maintainer would develop the following test plan *prior* to making any design or code changes. To be effective, test planning must occur during the same time frame as system release planning (Figure 9.4).

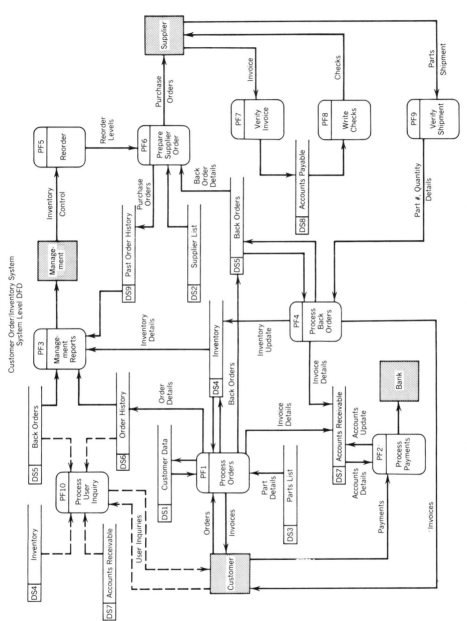

Customer Order/Inventory System
System Level DFD

Figure 9.3 Revised ACE Co. system data flow

187

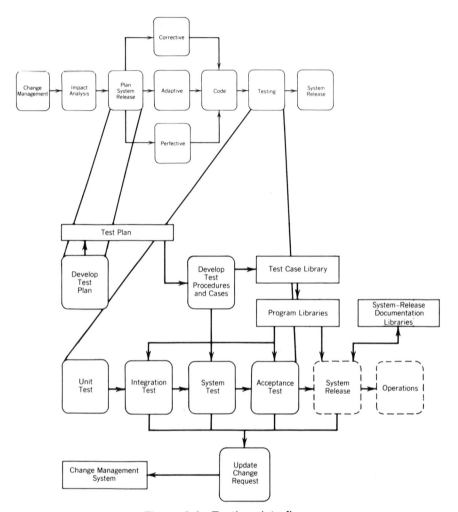

Figure 9.4 Testing data flow

188

SAMPLE TEST PLAN

Software Test Plan
for the
ACE Co. Billing System
Release 3, 1986
March 15, 1986
Prepared for:
Department / Contracting Agency
Prepared by:
Department / Contractor

SAMPLE TEST PLAN (continued)

Table of Contents

Overview of the test plan: This System Test Plan describes Release 3, 1986 of the ACE Billing System. The major enhancements contained in this release include:

Change Request No.	Description
8602-006	On-Line Customer Inquiry System

Schedule: Payroll System schedule—Release 3, 1986:

Unit test start date:	Feb. 1, 1986
Integration test start date:	March 1, 1986
System test start date:	March 20, 1986
Acceptance test start date:	April 1, 1986
Release date:	April 15, 1986
Installation date:	April 20, 1986

Human testing: The following work products will require formal walkthroughs or inspections:

Requirements: Inquiry subsystem requirements

Design: ACE Billing System—system design

Code: Inquiry subsystem code modules
Management Reports (PF3)
Process Orders (PF1)

Unit test: All new and revised modules will conform to the following:

Requirements: Test each unit using normal, extreme, and errone-ous input types using test cases of both the black and white box variety (grey box).

Test each unit for error detection and error recovery, including error messages.

Test all executable statements at least once and all structural test paths.

Responsibility: Programmer developing or revising each code module

Schedule: Following code inspection, not later than March 1, 1986.

Integration test: etc.

191

2.3. Test Procedures

Test procedures describe methods, or procedures for conducting walk-throughs and computer tests. For example, the test procedure for a requirements test could include the following:

- Inputs:
    Requirements document
    Change request
    System design document
- Process:
    Requirements walk-through with the user, senior technician, and manager present.
- Outputs:
    Modified functions identified and documented
    Approval/sign-off

For system testing, it might describe any pre-test procedures, equipment preparation (for hardware changes), software preparation (getting products out of integration test), and other processes (regression testing) that are required and the expected ouputs.

Test procedures simply describe how to conduct each of the incremental tests under the test plan.

2.4. Test Cases

Test cases describe the data to execute a test and the expected results. For example, an adaptive maintenance request to add a 2 digit vendor code to an equipment masterfile system might include the following test cases:

Test Case	Expected Results
Two numerics	Update equipment master file
Two alphabetics	Error processing
Two special characters	Error processing
Two blanks	Zero fill vendor code on equipment master file

The key difference between a well and poorly run test program is the ability to plan effectively for all phases of testing and to translate the plans into a productive test structure. This means that:

- Plans are developed early when sufficient time is available to develop tools and procedures (typically concurrent with system release planning—see Chapter 4).
- All test activities are preplanned and orchestrated through the person responsible for testing.
- The flow of data between each test level and between organizational lines is well defined.
- Managerial and technical responsibilities for each product are clearly specified.
- Test and integration structures are tailored to the size, complexity, and nature of the application.
- Project review and inspection procedures are rigorously applied.

3. TESTING TYPES

There are two types of testing: human and computer. The key features of each type are described in this section.

3.1. Human Testing

Walk-throughs, or inspections, are human tests. Walk-throughs assess the correctness of changes to requirements, specifications, designs, and code. Walk-throughs are the first check of quality and correctness. As shown in Figure 9.5, defects found during requirements, design, or code are inexpensive to correct.

The time and cost savings accumulate from:

- Fewer computer runs.
- Less debugging of incorrect results or failures.
- Less redesign and rework of requested changes.
- Less complicated future changes.
- Less corrective maintenance.

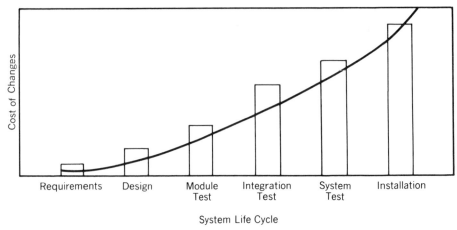

Figure 9.5   Cost of correcting defects during a scheduled release

Inspections and walk-throughs can find up to 80% of all defects (Brooks 1975). So use human testing as a major force in the incremental testing and quality assurance of revised programs.

3.2.   Computer Testing

Computer testing includes all machine-executable tests at the unit, integration, system, and acceptance levels. The relationship among test levels is shown in Figure 9.6. Computer testing begins with the inspected code, at the unit test level, and continues up through the user's acceptance of the revised system.

3.2.1.   Unit Test   Unit testing is the process of testing individual modules, subprograms, or subroutines in a program. Unit tests compare the function of a module to the revised functional specifications. The major unit testing activities are:

- Design test cases to exercise the new or revised code.
- Test the module.
- Compare the module's outputs—at the module's interface and any external files—to known results for each test case.
- Debug any problems using the problem-solving process described in Chapter 5.

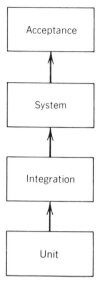

Figure 9.6 Bottom-up computer testing

- Repair the defect, and repeat the process until the unit passes testing.
- Update the change request to reflect the module's unit-tested status.

3.2.2. *Integration*   Integration testing pulls together the unchanged and revised modules for each program and tests their interfaces and the outputs from each program individually. The major integration testing activities are:

- Test the entire program using all of the test cases for each module and any others required at this level.
- Debug any problems using the problem-solving process described in Chapter 5.
- Update the change request to reflect the module's integration-tested status.

3.2.3. *System Test*   The system test verifies that system requirements, including all changes, have been satisfied. The major system testing activities are:

- Test programs and interfaces between programs (human, data bases, and files) to ensure that the system meets all original requirements plus the added changes. Regression testing is used to ensure that changes did not introduce new problems into the system before release.

- Compare results of the system test to the requirements. Programs that fail are returned, with the change request, to maintainers for correction.
- Maintainers identify and correct the errors. Problem causes are reflected on the change request.

3.2.4. Acceptance Test The user may specify the need for an acceptance test using live data in a live environment. The acceptance test should be planned for as any other test level.

3.3. When to Stop Testing

Because computer testing is an iterative process, it can be difficult to determine exactly when to stop testing. The following guidelines can help you make this decision:

- When time runs out (this is typical but not the best method of operation).
- When all test cases have been exercised without detecting errors.
- When all paths through the code have been tested at least once.
- When no additional errors are found.
- When defects found per tester drops below a certain rate per day (Figure 9.7). Lots of defects are found quickly, but level off at some point.
- When a certain percentage of the expected errors has been found. This assumes that you can project the error rate per 100 lines of code, or by function point or other size metrics (Chapter 8).
- When a certain percent of all expected errors has been found (Figure 9.8). The number of errors detected over time during unit, integration and system testing tend to follow an exponential curve (e.g., many at first, then fewer, and finally trickling off).

    By tracking error detection during a three-week system-testing period, you can determine what percentage of the total errors are found each day. If the daily total drops to 2 of 200 for several days, then you have reached a 99% level of test completion. If the daily total stays at 20, you've only reached a 90% level. This level of com-

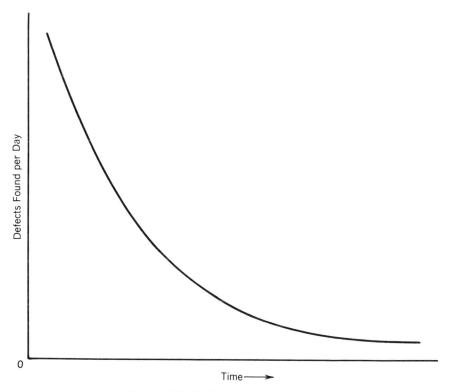

Figure 9.7 Defects found per tester

pletion can be specified beforehand, depending on the criticality of the system.

It isn't cost-effective to test for 100% defect-free software. Therefore choose a level of testing that is cost-effective for the underlying software.

For example, batch or noncritical systems need less testing. Real-time and critical systems such as a mission computer on a DOD platform (plane, submarine, ship, tank, etc.) require more exhaustive testing.

4. TESTING STRATEGIES

Effective planning is a necessary first step to a sound testing program. Another important area is selecting the right testing strategy. There are a number of strategies that can be applied to computer testing. They may

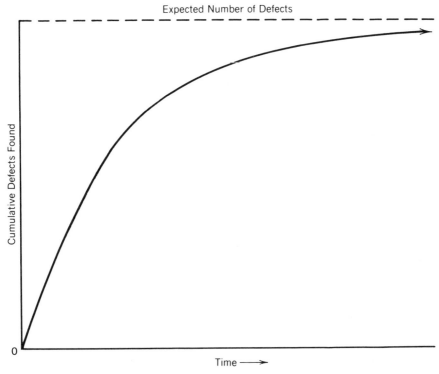

Figure 9.8   Percentage of errors found

be implemented individually or in various combinations. The strategies are:

- Black box testing
- White box testing
- Gray box testing
- Top-down testing
- Bottom-up testing

In this section we describe the features of each strategy.

4.1.   Black Box

Black box testing ensures that a program performs its functions as required. Black box test cases can be built as soon as the requirements are approved. The tester needs to know nothing about the internals of the program being tested, hence the name "black box." Maintainers develop test cases based on the functions to be performed. The code is tested using the maximum and minimum boundary values for each data item. Both valid and invalid values should be tested. For example:

- The requirements specify that net pay should be $0.00 to $99,999.99 (boundary values). Black box values would be -2000.00, -0.01, 0.00, 1000.00, 99,999.99, and 100,000.00.

Black box tests are developed as follows:

- Analyze requirements.
- List required functions.
- Identify modules or programs that perform the function.
- Develop test cases with boundary values to test each function.

4.2. White Box

White box test cases can only be built *after* the code (or pseudocode) is available. White box testing uses the program design, pseudocode, and code to create test cases for complete coverage of each decision (IF, CASE, UNTIL, or WHILE) and all of the conditions within each decision (AND, OR, NOT)

There are three levels of white box testing:

- Logic
- Decision
- Multiple decision (or path) coverage

Logic coverage executes each *decision* at least once. Consider the following example. It can be tested with A = 2, B = 3.

```
IF A = 2 AND B = 3
   C = 3
ELSE
   F = 3
ENDIF
```

```
IF A = 3 OR B = 3
   D = 3
ELSE
   G = 3
ENDIF
```

Decision, or branch coverage executes each *decision path* at least once. The previous example can be tested with:

- Case 1 (A = 2, B = 3)
- Case 2 (A = 2, B = 2)

Path testing executes each *path* through the code at least once. The previous example can be tested with:

- Case 1 (A = 2, B = 3)
- Case 2 (A = 2, B = 2)
- Case 3 (A = 3, B = 2)

McCabe's (1976) cyclomatic complexity metric is used to determine the maximum number of structural test paths. To simplify the concept, think of cyclomatic complexity as equivalent to the number of test paths. Based on this metric, the number of test paths in a module is a sum of the number of decisions (IF, CASE, WHILE, UNTIL) and conditions (AND, OR, NOT) plus 1. As a formula it looks like the following, where TP equals test paths.

TP = IFs + CASEs + WHILEs + UNTILs + ANDs + ORs + NOTs + 1

In the previous example, this formula would have yielded five structural paths. However, because of the comparisons chosen, the number could be reduced to three.

4.3. Gray Box

Gray box testing combines the strategies of both black and white box testing. To ensure the maximum amount of test coverage:

- Develop black box test cases first, using the change request and revised requirements.

- Develop white box test cases from the code when it is available.
- Gray box testing assumes a top-down strategy.

4.4. Top-Down

Top-down testing works incrementally through a program or system, beginning at the top. It works as follows:

- Test top (or driver) module first:

- Use module stubs to test subordinate modules as they are developed:

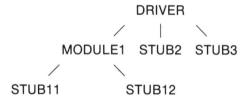

By using a top-down approach, errors can be localized to the tested modules, thereby reducing debugging time. Some additional benefits of top-down testing are that it:

- Produces better test coverage because the high-level modules are tested more often.
- Detects high-level design errors quickly before further implementation.
- Supports incremental delivery of products.
- Stubs are reusable.
- Testing gets easier as it proceeds.

4.5. Bottom-Up

As its name suggests, bottom-up testing begins with the lowest-level modules and works incrementally back up through the hierarchy.

Bottom-up testing is a useful technique when more than one programmer is working on a program change. Each programmer can code and test individual modules. Then modules can be set aside until all are ready for further testing.

Another advantage is that the lower-level, or worker, modules are tested more often. This is particularly useful if the lowest-level functions are the most complex.

The major disadvantage of bottom-up testing is that extensive rework may be required if the high-level logic was designed incorrectly. If changes have to be made, all modules may have to be changed.

5. TESTING TOOLS

Testing, especially as a full-time job, can be cumbersome and difficult without the right test tools. There are five categories of test tools:

- Data
- On-line
- Batch
- Documentation
- General

5.1. Types of Tools

Table 9.1 describes the features and best applications of each testing tool category.

5.2. Tool Costs

Various expenses are associated with implementing any tool. The costs include people, time, and money for:

- Product review and evaluation
- Management and technical approval
- Procurement—contracts and purchasing
- Product cost
- Installation
- Training—initial and periodic refresher
- Maintenance—annual maintenance

TABLE 9.1   Test tools by best application

Tools and Functions	Best Applications
Data	
Test data generators create test data from specifications	Black, white, and gray box testing
Structure and Data-flow analysis examines code to determine where the data comes from and goes to.	White box testing
Test case libraries automate maintenance of existing test cases and data	All testing
Data comparison utilities compare results of previous and current tests	Regression testing
On-line	
Module drivers execute lower-level modules	Unit testing structured modules
Network simulators simulate a network of users, using a script of transactions for interactive systems	Testing interactive or on-line systems
Batch	
Execution trace lists functions and subroutines executed	Difficult debugging situations
Execution/performance monitors count number of times each statement is executed, and the efficiency of execution	Testing efficiency problems and logic problems in loops
Program instrumentation reports data changes during processing	Integration testing, and when on-line drivers cannot be used
Documentation	
Spelling checkers eliminate spelling and stylistic problems	All documentation
Readability analysis determines fog index and improves comprehension	All documentation
Change marking identifies changes from previous documentation	All documents
General	
Compliers find syntax errors and supply cross-reference listings	Compilable languages
File formating and dump tools print program-to-program files in a readable format	All testing
Dump analysis and formatting print octal or hexadecimal dumps in a readable format	All testing
Static analysis automates analysis of quality and identification of possible problem areas for investigation and resolution	Error-prone modules
Emulators simulate different hardware and software environments, using more powerful systems	Real-time, embedded systems and micro-computer development and maintenance
Error data collection tracks all tests, failures, execution time, access time, and a host of other measurement data	System test

- Support—consulting, help line testing tools are not inexpensive, but provide a productive way of dealing with 50% of the evolution process.

6. SUMMARY

Testing is the process of examining documentation, or code, or executing a program with the intent of finding errors. A test that finds an error *is* a successful test.

The major differences between testing in development and maintenance environments are:

- Only changes need to be reviewed, not the entire product.
- Only new test cases that exercise the change need to be developed. They can then be added to the existing test bed.
- Only the existing test cases associated with changed products, along with any new test cases, will be needed to test the changes.
- Test results can be mechanically compared against previous test results to identify variations in the output caused by the changes. This comparison process is commonly known as regression testing.

Some guidelines for when to stop testing are when:

- Time runs out (this is the typical, but not the best, method of operation).
- All test cases have been exercised without detecting errors.
- All paths through the code have been tested at least once.
- No additional errors are found.
- The number of defects found per tester drops below a certain rate per day.
- A certain percentage of the expected errors has been found.
- A certain percentage of errors has been found.

Test planning ensures the desired focus on testing and is consistent with the top-down approach to batching change requests. Test planning ensures that tests are done incrementally to minimize defects and reduce the amount of corrective maintenance.

Some advantages of incremental testing are:

- Enables testing to begin early.
- Requires less work, not more work.
- Programming errors are detected earlier.
- Debugging is easier because the extent or domain of any problem is restricted.
- Testing is more thorough.
- Improved resource scheduling.

The three major test planning products are test plans, procedures, and cases. The key difference between a well and poorly run test program is the ability to plan effectively for all phases of testing and to translate the plans into a productive test structure. This means that:

- Plans are developed early when sufficient time is available to develop tools and procedures (typically concurrent with system release planning—see Chapter 4).
- All test activities are preplanned and orchestrated through the person responsible for testing.
- The flow of data between each test level and between organizational lines is well defined.
- Managerial and technical responsibilities for each product are clearly specified.

The major testing strategies are:

- Black box testing
- White box testing
- Gray box testing
- Top-down testing
- Bottom-up testing

The major test tools are:

- Data
- On-line
- Batch

- Documentation
- General

Following testing, the final software maintenance activity is to package the system and programs for release.

DISCUSSION QUESTIONS

1. What are some of the risks of skipping requirements, design, and code walk-throughs or inspections?

2. What are some of the risks of skipping unit and integration testing?

3. What are some guidelines for conducting more productive walk-throughs?

4. How will top-down, incremental testing help you deliver higher-quality programs?

5. How can bottom-up development and testing be used?

6. What are the dangers of bottom-up testing?

7. Which of the tools described in the reading do you use regularly, and how do they help you test your system?

CHAPTER

10

System Release and Configuration Management

Following successful system and acceptance tests, the final software maintenance activity packages and releases the revised software and documentation. One of the keys to a successful system release is configuration management—how you control and find all of the parts that make up the system. Think of it as an inventory control system for software and documentation.

Many maintainers see configuration management as an annoyance, but where you store the documents, code, and executable software can simplify or nullify all of your maintenance efforts. This chapter describes the objectives of system release, the release process, and the benefits of configuration management.

1. SYSTEM RELEASE

Releasing a system (Figure 10.1), once all scheduled maintenance work is complete, should be a simple process. With small systems, managed by a

207

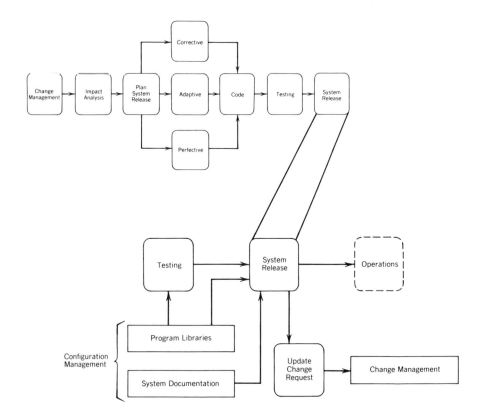

Figure 10.1　System-release data flow

single programmer, it is. But all systems grow. At some point they become too large to be managed by a single person. When you release
hundreds, perhaps thousands, of programs with reams of documentation,
there has to be excellent control to deliver all the right pieces to all of the
right people.

The objectives of system release are:

- Package the system for release.
- Deliver the system to the user.

The major system release activities to accomplish these goals are:

1. Expand and revise system release document (described in Chapter
4).

2. Package the system release, including all documentation, software, training, and other products of the maintenance process, as well as hardware if applicable.

3. Deliver or release the system to your clients.

4. Install the system release with backout procedures in case of serious failure.

The following example shows the completed system release document for the ACE Co. example that has been carried throughout the text.

SAMPLE RELEASE DOCUMENT

System Release Document
for the
ACE Co. Billing System
Release 3, 1986
March 15, 1986
Prepared for:
Client Relations Department
Prepared by:
Jay Arthur

SAMPLE RELEASE DOCUMENT (continued)

Table of Contents

SAMPLE RELEASE DOCUMENT (continued)

**Overview of the
system release:**
This System Release Document describes Release 3, 1986 of the ACE Billing System. The major enhancements contained in this release include:

Change Request No.	Description
8602-006	Customer Inquiry System Enhancement

Schedule:
ACE Billing System schedule—Release 3, 1986:

Design start date:	Nov. 1, 1985
Code start date:	Dec. 15, 1985
Unit test start date:	Feb. 1, 1986
Integration test start date:	March 1, 1986
System test start date:	March 20, 1986
Acceptance test start date:	April 1, 1986
Release date:	April 15, 1986
Installation date:	April 20, 1986

Specific products:

Documents: Order History Data Base Design   Attachment 1

This attachment describes all of the changes made to the Order History Data Base and any operational considerations caused by the changes.

ACE Billing System Operations Guide   Attachment 2

This attachment describes the changes to the ACE Billing System design and any operational considerations caused by the changes.

ACE Inquiry System User's Guide   Attachment 3

This attachment describes the procedures to inquire against the ACE data bases.

SAMPLE RELEASE DOCUMENT (continued)

ACE Billing System run procedures:

Run procedures are included in the System Release Document to identify all operational revisions by program caused by the release; e.g., additional files that need to be processed, JCL changes, error handling procedures.

Inquiry	Attachment 4
Management Reports	Attachment 5
Process Orders	Attachment 6

ACE Billing System design

Programs: ACE Billing program and module designs for the following programs.

Programs Released	Release Date	Install Date	Operational Changes
Inquiry	04/15/86	04/20/86	New
Process	04/15/86	04/20/86	No
Reports	04/15/86	04/20/86	No

Change requests: Release 3 change requests   Attachment 7

List of all changes included in release 3.

Notes: All questions or concerns regarding Release 3, 1986 of the ACE Billing System should be directed to the Project Manager on (212)555-5555.

Appendixes:

ACE Billing System Job Control	Appendix A
ACE Billing System Data Base	Appendix B
Document Distribution Listing	Appendix C

In the case of the ACE Co. billing system, there were only three programs and a handful of documents to release. But there were many revised designs, new designs for the inquiry system, new code modules for INQUIRY, and a host of related changes. Keeping track of all of the parts of the billing system (shown in Figure 10.2) is a job for configuration management.

2. CONFIGURATION MANAGEMENT

Tracking the request for the inquiry sub-system ensured that the system release went well. Another important part of change control is to manage the different versions of system products delivered to the users. *Configuration management* (Figure 10.3) handles the control of all products/ configuration items and changes to those items. Products/configuration items include documents, software, source code, hardware, tapes, disks, and computer listings.

Many people consider configuration management to be a roadblock, a part of the job they simply tolerate. In reality configuration management plays a major role in ensuring the quality of the delivered system and the productivity of the system maintainers. Configuration management should not be taken lightly. It ensures that approved products are not contaminated by uncontrolled or unapproved changes.

The objectives of configuration management are to:

- Uniquely identify every version of every product/configuration item.
- Retain historical versions of software and documentation.
- Provide an audit trail of all changes.

There are a number of reasons for such strict control of software and documentation components:

1. Changes are auditable. In case of legal action, changes must be traceable from the final product back through all of the interim products and workers to the original change request. Computer legislation has made this an essential management goal.

2. It helps ensure quality, and quality software needs less maintenance. Without configuration management it is easy to send out a wrong or bad version of a computer program or its documentation.

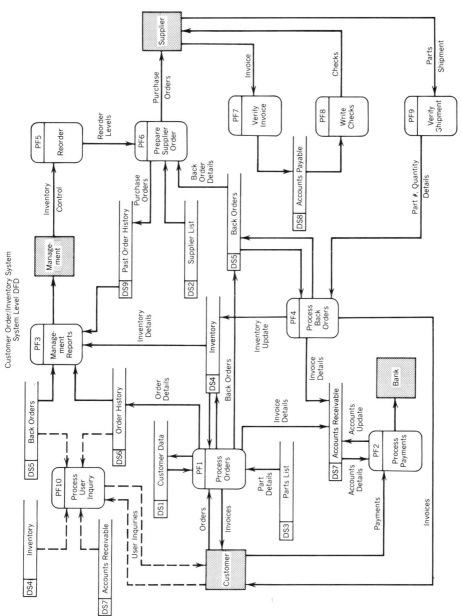

Customer Order/Inventory System
System Level DFD

Figure 10.2 Revised ACE Co. system data flow

215

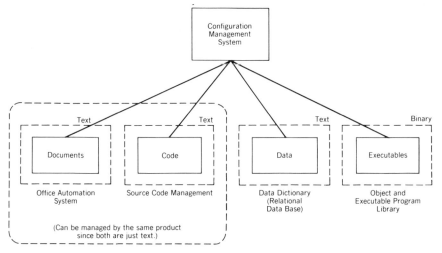

Figure 10.3   A complete configuration management system

3. It helps improve productivity. Programmers and analysts know exactly where to go to find any piece of the system. Knowing where to find another programmer's code and documentation at 3 A.M., when he or she is on vacation in the south of France, is a godsend.

To garner these benefits, you have to decide which items to control.

2.1. Configuration Items

As shown in Figure 10.3, you will need to control documentation, code, data, executable software, and any other products, such as training or hardware. There are many different ways that this can be done, manually (yech!) or mechanically.

Each item has to be in a common place where everyone, who has the authority, can access it and close to the person or machine that uses it. For example, consider Figure 10.4. Documents are manually maintained in a library close to the programmer/analyst, while code, data, and executable software are managed in the target computer. For small installations this is sufficient.

In a larger installation, code, data, and documents can be managed in a main computer or a separate system (Figure 10.5) that is oriented toward *text* manipulation. The host machine is designed for testing executable programs and processing data, not editing. UNIX™ provides such a distributed environment.

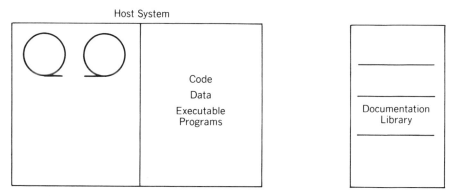

Figure 10.4 Manual and automated configuration management

There are many advantages to such an environment: quick response time, reliability of the smaller system, ability to expand in small increments (buying smaller systems instead of larger, more expensive host systems), and increased productivity from expanded, higher-quality computer systems. You might notice that in this environment, however, some minor editing of code must be done in the host environment during debugging.

In a more advanced environment (Figure 10.6), each programmer/ analyst would have a personal computer that connects to the host (for compiling and testing) and to the smaller machine. The personal computer maximizes productivity when editing—editing is up to 70% of a maintainer's effort. The host computer maximizes productivity for compiling and testing. The smaller machines provide a *common* area for

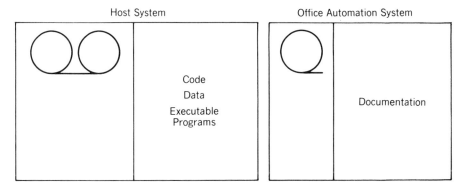

Figure 10.5 Automated documentation

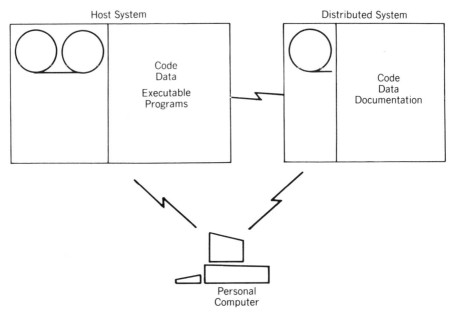

Figure 10.6   Fully integrated configuration management system

storing documents, code, data, and graphics, and they enable electronic communications among the maintenance staff.

The personal computer, however, is not a good place to store any of the work products. Why? Because it is accessible by only one person at a time. You need a *central, common* place to store these items.

To establish which of these environments are right for your application and how you should manage your work products, you need to identify the configuration management activities required.

2.2. Configuration Management Activities

The activities are simple; implementing them takes time and money. They are:

- Defining the configuration (what products go where).
- Establishing change control.
- Linking change control to configuration management.
- Tracking changes to the configuration.

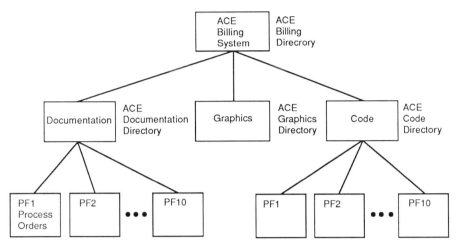

Figure 10.7 Directory organization of ACE Co. text

Documents might go into a library, or they might be stored on a computer system. If they reside in a computer, they are a lot like code—they can be stored in a magnetic library or managed by a software configuration management system. On an IBM system, they could be stored in a PDS, partitioned data set. Under UNIX or MS-DOS™ they might be stored under a directory (Figure 10.7). Data should be managed by some form of data dictionary.

Executable object modules and programs should have separate libraries for each testing and release activity (Figure 10.8). To retain configura-

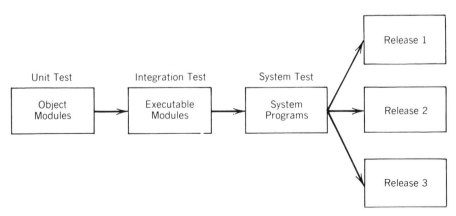

Figure 10.8 Binary configuration management of testing phases and system releases

tion control, the integration test cannot randomly dump programs into the system test library, any more than the system test can copy programs over previous releases.

It takes organization and planning to ensure that the right configuration items make it to release. Change management must couple with configuration management to make this happen. This can be done manually or, preferably, mechanically.

Finally, there must be a method of examining all work products to identify what has been changed. Again, this can be a manual or mechanical process, which leads us to a discussion of tools.

2.3. Configuration Management Tools

There are several different types of products that must be managed, giving rise to several different types of tools. Those types of products are:

- Text—documents and code
- Graphics
- Data
- Binary—object and executable code

2.3.1. Text.   On IBM, text can be managed in a PDS, or with automated systems like LIBRARIAN, PANVALET, or CCC. On UNIX, text can be well managed with SCCS (Source Code Control System). Similar products exist for other software environments.

2.3.2. Graphics.   Most graphics, because of the format of their files, are managed by the software systems that produce them. In general, they are not compatible with text management systems.

2.3.3. Data.   Data has to be put together and referenced in so many ways that only a data dictionary will satisfy the needs of all users. There are many such products. Pick one.

2.3.4. Binary.   There are many products for managing binary products as well. I recommend that you choose one that works with a change management system. In IBM, that leads you to CCC or the PANSOPHICS array of PANVALET, PANEXEC (binary), and CMS (Change Management System). By the time this book is published, there will be other equally competitive systems. Under UNIX, SCCS mates with CMTS (Change Management Tracking System). Executable programs can be easily maintained under the UNIX directory structures.

Your task is to choose among the many available systems and methods to control the configuration of the software, data, and documentation that make up each system release.

3. SUMMARY

The last software evolution activity is system release. It packages all of the deliverable products for delivery to the client. It has two simple objectives:

- Package the system for release.
- Deliver the system to the user.

The major system release activities to accomplish these goals are:

1. Complete the system release document.
2. Package the system release.
3. Deliver the system.
4. Install the system.

The successful completion of a system release depends on configuration management, whose objectives are to:

- Uniquely identify every configuration item (CI).
- Retain historical versions of CIs.
- Provide an audit trail of all changes.

This ensures:

- Changes are auditable.
- System quality.
- Maintainer productivity.

Configuration management must work in concert with change management to control changes to:

Text—documentation and code

Graphics

Data

Object and executable code

This chapter has identified ways to automate and manage changes to the products of the software maintenance process. The next chapter will deal with implementing a cohesive, productive, software evolution environment.

DISCUSSION QUESTIONS

1. What are the strengths and weaknesses of your existing configuration management and system release process?

2. What can be done to improve those weaknesses.

3. Why is configuration management one of the cornerstones of high-quality, productive software maintenance?

4. How can you streamline your existing system release process?

CHAPTER

11

Implementing Software Evolution

Software evolution, as described in the preceding chapters, is a critical business function. Most organizations depend on existing software systems for their revenue and continued operation.

To offset an increasing demand and a growing software inventory, improvements are needed in the skills and productivity of maintainers and in the quality and effectiveness of their work. Providing maintainers with the latest knowledge, skills, and techniques to achieve their mission is the aim of this book.

I recognize that not all system maintainers are created equal, but that they can be educated to equivalent skill levels given the tools and methods that facilitate each maintenance activity. The difference between the best and worst performers is an order of magnitude. The best maintainers can execute the key software maintenance activities more effectively than their counterparts. No single activity, or area of expertise accounts for the differences. The key is to do most things a little better, say, 5–10% better. A little more knowledge and skill multiplied over many activities produces striking differences in performance.

223

Software evolution has a few key goals:

1. To reduce corrective maintenance as much as possible. Correcting defects that could have been *prevented* is expensive and wasteful.
2. To maximize the productivity of adaptive maintenance. Enhancements deliver more benefit to the user. The more time we have for enhancements, the better.
3. To initiate high-yield perfective maintenance activities to help meet the preceding two goals and minimize maintenance costs.

1. CRITICAL SUCCESS FACTORS

To meet these goals the following activities are critical to the success of maintaining software productively. These factors were referred to as critical success factors throughout the text. The critical success factors are:

1. Develop and adhere to a well-defined, structured maintenance process.
2. Use structured design and coding principles:

   Unless structured methods are applied to maintenance work, quality suffers causing software failures and rework.

   Corrective and adaptive maintenance cost more without a structured approach.

   Poor design and implementation cause early retirement and replacement of systems at a higher cost ($30/line of code versus $2/line for restructured code). There is as much as a 40:1 difference between replacement and maintenance costs (Pressman 1982). Without structured design and implementation of software changes, systems rapidly slide into unmaintainable obsolescence.
3. Control software products and capture data about the software maintenance process through change management and configuration management systems:

   Maintainers can lose changes without change and configuration management, causing rework.

   Corrective maintenance costs are higher without them, because the quality missing from delivered software causes a higher incidence of corrective changes following a system release.

4. Conduct an impact analysis of all requested changes before agreeing to action them:

Low estimates result from poor evaluation of impacts. Schedule overruns and higher costs result from improper estimates. In a contract environment, loss of revenue can result if changes are incorrectly estimated.

Inadequate evaluations lead to a higher frequency of corrective maintenance. Correcting or adapting only the programs directly affected by a change often cause related programs to fail in actual operation of the system.

5. Establish scheduled releases and batch change requests:

Lower system quality results from working spurious, frequent, and uncontrolled changes. Testing cannot be planned and executed to minimize defects.

Reduced productivity stems from the inability to batch changes to a program or module. This forces the maintainer to relearn the design and code each time a new change is required, rather than once for several grouped changes.

6. Add quality to every design and piece of code touched:

Maintainers cannot become more productive without quality improvements. Maintenance productivity is a direct function of the quality of the existing system. Productivity can only improve if the quality of the existing system improves.

7. Gather quality assurance data, and use it to refine software development and maintenance practices:

There is no good way to get better at software maintenance without examining where problems and successes have occurred in the past.

Maintainers are unable to produce more and better work without definitive measurements that identify the methods and tools that facilitate productivity and quality.

No forum exists for sharing the knowledge of super programmers without careful study of what they do that is different from the ordinary programmers.

8. Use incremental testing throughout the software maintenance process to improve the quality of delivered software:

Reliability problems occur when system is released but not thoroughly tested.

Rework costs are high because defects are missed. Incremental testing drives out more defects because of its iterative examination of requirements, designs, and code.

9. Introduce and use modern, automated tools to improve quality and productivity:

Productivity is limited by manual methods. Automated tools improve the quality of actions taken and thereby improve productivity.

Quality is compromised because "to err is human." Automated processes have less likelihood of failure or defect.

10. Obtain management's support:

It is difficult to establish any programs to meet these critical success factors without management support. To implement these success factors requires money, time, and people, which management is loath to expend unless there is an obvious return on investment (see Chapter 12).

There is reduced political awareness of the importance of maintenance work. Maintained systems are the "cash cows" of any company. They've already been developed and are maturing with each maintenance release. Development work seems glamorous because of the production of an end product, but maintenance, when performed properly, is equally glamorous. It should be kept in management's view.

2. TYPES OF MAINTENANCE

Functionally, software maintenance can be divided into three categories: corrective, adaptive, and perfective.

Corrective   Corrective maintenance includes all changes required by defects. This type of maintenance focuses on correcting defects to keep the system operational. Corrective maintenance is often a reactive process. Defects generally need to be corrected immediately or in the near future. All corrective maintenance is related to the system not performing as originally intended, or as specified in the requirements.

Maintainers should seek to minimize the cost and

amount of corrective maintenance performed by *preventing* defects.

Adaptive   Adaptive maintenance includes all work related to changing the functionality of the software. The work is referred to as enhancements. Adaptive maintenance includes changes, additions, insertions, deletions, modifications, extensions, and enhancements that are made to a system to meet the evolving needs of the user and the environment in which the system must operate. Adaptive maintenance is generally performed as a result of new, or changing requirements.

Maintainers should seek to maximize the productivity and quality of this *evolutionary* form of software maintenance.

Perfective   Perfective maintenance includes all efforts to augment the quality of the software. Perfective maintenance includes restructuring code, updating documentation, improving reliability or efficiency, and many other activities discussed in Chapter 7.

At least 5% of the staff should be allocated initially to perfective maintenance and create a PM staff to handle the tough problems. It takes some skill.

If you can't do this, integrate perfective maintenance with enhancements to restructure the code inexpensively during the maintenance process.

3. SOFTWARE DEVELOPMENT

This section describes how software maintenance is affected by software development. It then describes ways to reduce software maintenance costs for each of the three types of maintenance during development.

The software life cycle covers the period from system conception to retirement. There are many definitions of the software life cycle. They differ primarily in the classifications of phases and activities. One traditional definition is:

- Requirements definition
- Preliminary design
- Detailed design

- Implementation
- Testing
- Operation and maintenance

The software life cycle phases directly influence the quality of the delivered system, and hence its maintainability. There are some general ways of *developing* systems to minimize its maintenance costs:

- Use prototyping to define and test requirements quickly.
- Establish and enforce software engineering standards that include maintenance.
- Include quality and maintenance objectives in the requirements specification.
- Use people with maintenance experience in the development of the product; they know how to avoid doing things that adversely affect maintainability.
- Rotate development people into maintenance to get that experience. Strictly development programmers rarely know how to build easy-to-maintain software.
- Standardize data using data design and data dictionaries. Use data base techniques and define data in third-normal-form to minimize redundancy and maximize maintainability.
- Use structured design and programming (I hope this is self-explanatory).
- Use automated tools to provide standard boiler plate for all documents and code, to measure code quality, to restructure code, and to manage the system's configuration and changes to the software.
- Use the highest-level language possible (i.e., assembler is not as maintainable and portable as a third-generation language like ADA, C, or COBOL; use a fourth-generation language if possible).
- Strive for machine independence.
- When designing the new system, anticipate future developments in hardware, telecommunications, and system software that will improve maintenance of the system (e.g., standard transmission protocols).
- Employ some form of quality inspection and control.
- Use available compiler library routines, like sort or sine, and design and build as many reusable modules as possible to minimize the

amount of code that must be maintained. Use skeletons of *proven logic* to implement any of the remaining modules. Up to 80% of any system can be reused (Kapur 1982). Keep these reusable routines stored in the configuration management system so that:

They can be listed and found easily.

The CM system can monitor the amount of reusable code actually used.

The CM system can maintain a cross reference of module usage.

If a system is developed with maintainability, flexibility, and reliability in mind, it will evolve easily and last longer before sinking into obsolescence. Maintenance begins when the user accepts the software system. Following acceptance, corrections and enhancements escalate as the user gains complete understanding of the delivered system.

Software evolution begins when the user requests a change, and it ends when the user accepts the modified system and documentation. Therefore one way of describing the software maintenance activities is to define them as iterations of the first five steps of the software life cycle. There are numerous ways to reduce maintenance costs during a system release.

4. SOFTWARE EVOLUTION

To begin to determine how to build a software evolution environment, let's apply a Pareto analysis to the software life cycle. Improvements should be focused on the work that costs the most or needs the most attention. Consider the following chart of maintenance costs:

Survey	Year	Maintenance (%)
Canning	1972	60 (Canning 1972)
Boehm	1973	40–80 (Boehm 1973)
DeRose & Nyman	1976	60–70 (DeRose 1978)
Mills	1976	75 (Mills 1976)
Zelkowitz	1979	67 (Zelkowitz 1979)
Cashman & Holt	1979	60–80 (Cashman 1980)

These references all agree that maintenance is 60–80% of the current software expense. From our Pareto analysis we see that we should focus most of our resources on improving maintenance, not development! The following suggestions provide avenues for improvement in the three types of maintenance: corrective, adaptive, and perfective.

4.1. Corrective

- Use high-level languages (low-level languages are for machines; high-level languages are for people).
- Keep modules small, modular, and simple (they are easier to understand and fix).
- Use structured techniques.
- Use on-line testing and diagnostic tools.
- Use tools (i.e., test data generators) to maximize test coverage.
- Use reusable code modules and library routines wherever possible (these are invariably more widely tested and reliable).
- Use Pareto analysis (Chapter 7) to identify those programs or modules incurring the most corrective maintenance and restructure or rewrite them to fix their reliability problems permanently.

4.2. Adaptive

- Use a standard, high-level language that is also portable (ADA, ANSI COBOL, C, etc.). Use higher-level languages where feasible.
- Strive for hardware independence (to minimize environmental changes). An example of hardware independence is when assembler language programmers moved programs from IBM's MVS/OS to MVS/XA and discovered that some programs trickily used the unused 16 bits of the PSW (Program Status Word) for temporary storage. Under XA, however, the operating system used the entire PSW, and programs that worked under OS would abend under XA and sometimes crash the entire operating system.
- Isolate the system-dependent code in independent modules (input/output, operating system calls, etc.).
- Isolate external interfaces by modules (i.e., terminal handling routines).
- Identify and plan for future environments as they become known.
- Prototype major enhancements.
- Let the user format outputs using fourth-generation report generators.

- Identify and plan for future user needs.
- Identify perfective maintenance candidates that incur the most costly enhancements and correct them. Remember only 5–10% of all code suffers these continuous changes. Move decisions and data into tables, modularize, and so forth, to minimize maintenance costs.
- Develop on-line tutorials and help screens to minimize trouble reports.
- Use technical writers to develop documentation.
- Track those areas where human factors are the majority of the defects and improve the documentation and training to help the user.

4.3. Perfective

Only improve modules that:

- Have a high usage level (CPU time, clock time, connect time, etc.).
- Have a reasonable remaining life span (one-year minimum).
- Have a high cost for corrective or adaptive maintenance (see Pareto analysis in Chapter 7).

5. THE STATE OF SOFTWARE MAINTENANCE

Nolan (1979) described the six stages of data processing maturity:

1. *Initiation*—development of the first applications without adequate methodology or technology.
2. *Contagion*—increasing demand for software applications, coupled with enthusiastic development but poor planning.
3. *Control*—user and management frustration, where software maintenance is the major portion of the DP budget, and applications are backlogged.
4. *Integration*—the need to integrate existing applications, even though their current design prohibits such activities. Need for data base and decision support become apparent, and the effects of design on maintenance become apparent.
5. *Data administration*—strategic planning and data administration take hold and encourage development of maintainable systems. Extensive retrofitting of existing systems occurs.

6. *Maturity*—information engineering, development, and maintenance handled correctly and robustly.

To this list, I would add two steps:

1. *Measurement*—data gathering on all aspects of software engineering.
2. *Process control*—applying the measurement data to ensure the quality of evolving software.

6. EVOLUTION

Most data-processing organizations are currently in the control and integration phases. Others are involved in data administration and the prior four. To decide where to begin improving the software maintenance process you can:

- Shoot from the hip.
- Decide, honestly, where you are on the maturity ᴄ   ᴇ. Analyze the available data, formulate questionaires to gather data from the maintainers, and make some decisions about how to move to the next level of maturity and where to maximize the benefit (i.e., through a Pareto analysis; see Chapter 7).

     Management doesn't like to spend money without a return on investment. During the first phase of implementing a cohesive software maintenance environment, they will be looking for changes that demonstrably affect productivity and quality. Some up-front analysis will ensure that the most important projects are chosen and implemented. Once these have succeeded, management will be more willing to open up the purse strings for subsequent improvements.

Valuable information used to make these decisions are measurements:

- Change requests (by type, severity, document, system, program, module, hardware, telecommunications, or human factors).
- Hours worked (by system, program, module, document, or maintenance phase—requirements, design, code, test).
- Lines of code changed (by type of maintenance, system, program, or module).

- Module complexity.
- Maintenance productivity (Boehm 1981):

Maintenance productivity
= (Lines of code added, changed or deleted)/staff-months

You and your colleagues may have pet peeves that you would like to tackle first, but in the beginning, look for projects with:

- A high return on investment
- A quick payback
- A low initial investment

Perfective maintenance of a *major system component* that consumes a *significant portion* of your maintenance resources could be an excellent first project. It meets all of the preceding goals.

For the long term, look at the change requests and time worked. Is there a problem with:

- Configuration management of documentation, code, data, object module, and executable programs?
- Controlling changes to the system?
- Lack of scheduled releases?
- The quality of developed systems?
- The methodology used for corrective and adaptive maintenance?
- Manual documentation, communication, or other processes and methods?
- Any of the other critical success factors?

Solving these problems takes longer to implement (i.e., six months to a year). They must be sold to both management and the programming staff. Implementing a configuration management, change control, or office automation system is like implementing any other software system; it takes time and resources.

Don't try to do all of these long-range changes at once; it is not possible because of time and resource constraints. It may take up to five years to implement all of these tools and methods. I know; I've done it. Using Pareto analysis, chose the highest priority improvement and:

- Initiate a proposal, just like you would a new development project.
- Get management approval and buy-in.
- Get programmer and analyst (user) input into the development and implementation of the system.
- Define requirements, including long-range quality and maintenance goals (i.e., how the configuration management system will integrate with the change control system or office automation system).
- Buy a package that meets your needs (it's cheaper than developing one; someone else has to maintain it for you).
- Train the managers, programmers, and analysts in its use just prior to implementation. If maintainers can't use the tool on the job, training value is lost within two months.
- If possible, try to avoid a mass conversion. Only train and implement the new tool with 30–50 people at a time. Hold their hand. Make them feel special. Ensure that they get the right training and support to ensure acceptance of the product or methodology.

  This also allows overlapping implementation of maintenance improvement projects where one group can be learning configuration management while another is learning change control. It will not take as long to implement the entire maintenance environment when done this way.
- Schedule the conversion to coincide with slack times in the maintenance group's work load. Don't try to convert them during the middle of a release. Under management orders, I've tried this. It doesn't work.
- Access the success of the initial implementation group, and revise the strategy and approach before converting the next group. Repeat this process until everyone is trained and satisfactorily involved with the project.
- If possible, measure improvements in quality and productivity before, during, and after the implementation of a tool or methodology. This helps quantify return on investment to both managers and programmers (Arthur 1985).
- Finally, analyze the results of the project several months after implementation. What did the people like or not like? How can you improve the implementation and acceptance of the next tool or method? Revise your plans accordingly, and start on the next project.
- Publish the results to develop an anticipation among the remaining staff and managers.

• Whenever possible, implement a few short-range projects, like perfective maintenance, that will show a quick return on investment. This helps the maintenance improvement program keep a high profile, management support, and continuous programmer awareness. This "Hawthorne effect" will improve acceptance and motivation.

7. SUMMARY

Software evolution and maintenance consists of the activities required to keep a software system operational and beneficial after it is accepted and placed into production.

This text used a seven-phase approach to represent the software maintenance process. Those phases are:

• Change management
• Impact analysis
• Plan system release
• Design changes
• Code changes
• Test changes
• Release the system

As previously described, there are three types of maintenance:

• Corrective maintenance, which includes all changes related to the system not performing as originally specified in the requirements.
• Adaptive maintenance, which includes all changes, additions, insertions, deletions, modifications, extensions, and enhancements that are made to a system to meet the evolving needs of the user and the environment in which the system must operate.
• Perfective maintenance, which includes all efforts to improve the quality of the software.

It is important to remember that the work can be divided functionally for discussion purposes, but much of it is performed concurrently and iteratively.

The critical success factors of software maintenance are:

- Develop and adhere to a well-defined and structured software maintenance methodology.
- Control software products, and capture data about the software maintenance process through change management and configuration management systems.
- Conduct an impact analysis of all requested changes before agreeing to action them.
- Establish scheduled releases and batch change requests.
- Use structured design and coding principles.
- Add quality to every design and piece of code touched.
- Gather quality assurance data, and use it to refine software development and maintenance practices.
- Use incremental testing throughout the software maintenance process to improve the quality of the delivered software.
- Introduce and use modern, automated tools to improve quality and productivity.
- Obtain management's support.

Once you establish a productive, high-quality environment for software evolution, your new and existing systems will continue to evolve effectively.

DISCUSSION QUESTIONS

1. Rank order the critical success factors according to their application in your environment.

2. Add any others you think are relevant.

3. Based on your knowledge of your current software-maintenance environment, identify the two best short- and long-term projects to undertake immediately to stimulate software evolution.

4. List, in order, other projects that you feel are essential to a productive, high-quality software maintenance environment.

12

Managing Software Evolution

No discussion of software evolution would be complete without some mention of managing the software evolution environment. The quality and productivity of software maintainers depends as much on good management as on any other aspect of the process. A manager who relies on magic technological solutions may be overlooking the simple, cost-effective answer of better management. As stated in Chapter 1, the key to productivity and quality gains is to do everything a little bit better; management is one of those things.

There are many problems that managers face when maintaining computer software. A few of them are:

- High overtime expenses for corrective maintenance.
- User's complaints about lack of responsiveness.
- Employee turnover.
- Feeling that maintenance is not as important as development.

- Productive maintainers are not rewarded like fire fighters (who fix program abends).
- Lack of adherence to standards.
- Lack of concern for quality assurance.
- Schedule slips that invariably shorten testing, and lead to downtime and overtime costs

These are perhaps the most common, but there are others. Take a moment to list your favorites. Think about them as you read the rest of this chapter.

1. SOFTWARE MAINTENANCE

Like software defects, these maintenance problems are *symptoms* of the problem, not the root, or *cause,* of the problem. Too often, we become accustomed to the status quo. We become immune to the problems. They seem to be a part of the process. Nonsense. Change the process.

To overcome these problems, the problem analysis section of Chapter 5 is useful for defining, isolating, and solving the cause of each problem. The key questions each manager has to ask are:

1. Why are we still doing corrective maintenance?

2. Why does adaptive maintenance get harder instead of easier?

3. How can we reduce the costs of maintenance?

Corrective maintenance is caused by defective software—software that was developed or maintained by people. This indicates a quality problem—a *lack of knowledge* by the builders or maintainers—not defective maintainers. Or it may be a problem with the process.

With superior programming methodologies and the vast array of tools at the command of system designers and developers, why are systems still built with bugs? To err is human. Quality problems are not solved by flogging programmers or by setting up a quality assurance group to police the errant coders. Quality problems are a lack of knowledge or understanding of how to perform correctly every step of software maintenance. It takes years to learn everything possible about proper maintenance. This book distills all of my years of knowledge about correcting, enhancing, and improving software. Let it serve as a guide to enhancing your staff's knowledge.

Why do managers, analysts, and programmers believe that corrective maintenance is inevitable? Status quo. After a period of time, we become saturated with defects, complex software, and problems. We cease to be able to evaluate the problem. Chrysler almost failed because of this myopia. Then in came Lee Iaccoca, who didn't have his blinders on. He listened to his workers; he tried crazy things. They brought Japanese cars into the plant to show the workers how well the doors, hoods, and trunks were hung; how the parts fitted together; how precise the engineering was in the drive train. Quality is not only possible; it's mandatory to survive in a competitive environment. Take the blinders off your staff and yourself.

Adaptive maintenance gets harder. The simple software with which you began is enhanced and corrected by legions of programmers in its life. Add this function. Add another. Add four more. Fix this. Fix that. The lack of understanding and knowledge of junior programmers has turned what may have been a simple system into a nightmare. To solve this problem, you have two choices: replacement or re-engineering.

How do we reduce the costs of enhancement and repair? Consider the following possibilities:

1. Do a better job of managing the development and maintenance of software to promote quality achievements to:

    Eliminate bugs before they have to be fixed.

    Deliver maintainable products.

    Focus on errors, sources of errors, and their elimination.

    Focus on quality, maintainability, ease of enhancement.

    Reward teams with the fewest problems in a new release.

2. Do a better job of building new programs and systems (see Chapter 11).

3. Do a better job of enhancing existing programs:

    Promote quality assurance by identifying common problems and training the development and maintenance staff to avoid such problems.

    Build structured, maintainable new modules, rather than integrate code into the existing spaghetti.

    Design and administer the data.

    Use structured maintenance techniques (scheduled releases).

4. Question the beliefs that:

> Corrective maintenance is inevitable.
>
> Zero defect software is an unreachable goal.
>
> Systems will always be "hard" to maintain.

2. SOFTWARE EVOLUTION OBJECTIVES

It should come as no surprise that software maintenance has a potentially high return on investment. It's far cheaper than replacement of existing systems. The following expenses from the Department of Defense give you some idea:

- 60 to 70% of DOD's software dollars are spent after software has been tested and delivered.
- The 1985 DOD software budget was $5 billion. This budget should grow to $20 billion in the 1990s.
- The General Accounting Office (GAO) estimates $1.3 billion for non-DOD maintenance (Couger 1985).

To meet the needs of software users, management has but a few simple objectives:

- Keep the system operational.
- Keep the users happy.
- Keep the staff happy.
- Maximize return on investment.
- Minimize costs.

How simple in concept, but how difficult to achieve. The following sections give simply stated solutions that should be implemented in a scheduled way. Chapter 7 explained how to use Pareto analysis to identify the best payback. Use it to choose among these alternatives and set a course beyond the scope of your blinded vision.

3. SOFTWARE DEVELOPMENT

The maintainability of a system is a direct result of how it was developed. For each of the phases of the software life cycle, implement the following:

Requirements Documentation

1. Select a minimal set that meets maintenance needs (complexity is the bane of documentation).

2. Standardize (simplifies reading and translation). Standards also reduce variation—the root of most defects.

3. Automate documentation (mechanize wherever possible).

Design

1. Require design walk-throughs and inspections.

2. Standardize design documentation.

3. Automate documentation.

Code

1. Build hierarchical programs from functional modules, reusing as many functions as possible. (Up to 80% of a given program's code is reusable.)

2. Require single functions to be in separate modules. Unstructured programs require four times as much maintenance effort as fully structured programs.

3. Limit module size. (Ninety-five percent of all modules should be under 100 ELOC or 10 decisions.)

4. Use single entry and single exit from each module.

5. Isolate hardware and software dependencies (i.e., type of hardware, operating system, and DBMS) to a few modules.

6. Ensure *data coupling* by passing only data items (not switches and flags) between modules.

7. Abolish self-modifying code (i.e., ALTER in COBOL).

8. Use data names for constants (i.e., pi = 3.14).

9. Restrict or eliminate GOTOs if the language supports all structured programming constructs (IF, CASE, DOWHILE, DOUNTIL).

10. Use documentation and comments. Each module should have:

    A header block to describe the program name/module name, processing (including inputs and outputs), assumptions, references (i.e., design documents).

    Comments at interface points (i.e., data passed, modified, and returned).

Comments around complex code or where code is not clear.

Variable names that are descriptive (corporate data administration should see to this).

Testing

1. Prevent defects by changing the software evolution process.

2. Find bugs before turning the system over to maintenance:

Use prototyping to reduce requirement and design problems.

Use incremental testing to ensure the quality of the developing system.

3. Build a test bed for maintenance work to use as a baseline.

4. SOFTWARE EVOLUTION

To maximize return on investment, prioritize and schedule changes (see Chapter 4). To minimize costs and maximize return on investment:

- Initiate perfective maintenance of high-cost software (see Chapter 7)
- Rewrite existing systems

Use the existing system as a prototype. Maintainers know what went wrong. Use them to build the new system. Choose systems for rewrites that are:

- Expensive to run (old hardware or BSP—before structured programming).
- Out-of-date technically (technicians tend to follow technology—high turnover rate).
- Expensive to maintain (i.e., person days per 1000 LOC).

Establish minimal requirements for:

1. Change control:

Change requests

Change review board

Quality control

2. Scheduled releases.

3. Configuration management.

5. SOFTWARE MAINTENANCE ORGANIZATION

Like any other work environment, software maintenance requires organization—teams of people working on specific aspects of the process, specialists who can focus and develop their abilities in each area. The organizations you will most likely need are:

Maintenance control center (trouble reporting center): to manage change requests.

Review board: to determine ROI and priorities on system change requests.

System design staff: small (1–4 people) to handle impact analysis, system release planning, and system design.

Design and implementation staff: to handle design, code, unit and integration tests.

System test organization: to test the system, thereby minimizing corrective maintenance and user frustration.

Quality assurance group: to determine causes of defects and reduced effectiveness, and to use this information to devise training and education to improve productivity and quality in development and maintenance. They can also select perfective maintenance candidates (Chapter 7).

Perfective maintenance group: to restructure selected modules and programs.

6. MOTIVATION

All of these organizations need motivation. For some reason, maintenance is not considered "good," fun, or rewarding. The following items give you clues about how to make, and keep, maintainers happy:

1. Maintenance has only 50–66% of motivating potential of other programming work (Couger 1985) because:

Such work is considered not challenging, even boring.

It is not as glamorous as new development with new technology. Management focus on maintenance can change this. But don't focus on fighting fires; focus on the maintenance groups that do everything right!

Maintenance does not often involve new training. (Use training and development work as rewards for successful maintenance.)

2. Fix-it activities are demotivating:

Programmers are not very good at fixing bugs (Yourdon 1979).

Programmers are usually fixing someone else's mistake, not their own.

3. Hard-to-learn systems and code are due to:

Poor or complex system design.

Poor or nonexistent documentation.

Code written before structured programming (BSP).

Code written in lower-level language (i.e., assembler).

Original designers having moved on (remaining overall system information is folklore).

Use Pareto analysis and perfective maintenance (Chapters 7–8) to resolve these quality problems.

4. The first few "structured" programs written by every programmer may be difficult to maintain (before they truly understand how to do it well).

If all of these problems point to the need for job enrichment, not just job enlargement—the addition of more maintenance work—what should you do?

1. Redesign the job.
2. Expand skill variety via training and new tools.
3. Increase identification with task (i.e., participation in scheduling and decision making).
4. Increase significance of task (i.e., associate benefits and ROI with each change).
5. Increase autonomy and entrepreneurship (i.e., ownership of programs, modules, tasks like testing).

To achieve these goals, focus on results you would like to achieve. If you focus attention on fire fighters, notice that corrective maintenance will *increase,* not decrease. Some of the things you might focus on instead include:

1. Fewest abends.

2. Fewest severity 1 and 2 CRs.

3. Amount of perfective maintenance performed.

4. Appropriate use of standards and tools.

Wherever the manager focuses, the maintainers will improve. The Hawthorne effect works, but you must be extremely careful what signals you give because they will be followed.

7. FIRST STEPS

To maximize your return on investment, focus on the *worst first*. Perform perfective maintenance on the worst programs (cost the most in resources) to reduce costs as quickly as possible.

When . . . one module of 800 lines, which accounted for 30% of the maintenance in the entire system [was rewritten]—the rest of the work could be done with the initial savings (Weinberg 1979).

Identify the cost for each segment of system maintenance (see Chapter 7). Be willing to invest in renovation. Use quality assurance to ensure better replacement code.

Keep a change request log:

1. Manual at first
2. Automate
3. Integrate with project management
4. Identify worst-first candidates

Embrace configuration management to control software and documentation (Chapter 10).

Develop and maintain a scheduled system release control procedure that:

1. Consolidates change requests for better resource usage.
2. Enriches maintainer's jobs.
3. Forces user to do more research before requesting changes.

4. Eliminates "squeaky wheel" and "good-old-boy" prioritization of changes.

5. Facilitates resource sharing and backup.

6. Allows better planning (Chapter 4).

7. Makes perfective changes as important as user-requested changes.

8. Allows for periodic review and examination.

Face the fact that if you don't start now, you will be in the same place years from now.

8. SUMMARY

Successful software evolution management depends on the continuing adjustment of management style, organization, motivation, and objectives. Gains in productivity and quality depend on managers as much as any other factor in software maintenance.

It is up to managers to initiate or subscribe to projects that will improve the software maintenance environment.

Software evolution is much like a computer program (Figure 12.1); it consists of inputs, processes, and outputs.

- The only way to improve the quality of the product is to improve the quality of the inputs or the process.

- The only way to increase productivity is to increase the number of inputs, or to automate or streamline (not shortcut) part of the process.

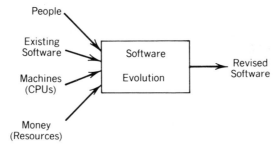

Figure 12.1 Inputs and outputs of software evolution

Many of these input and process adjustments have been described in this book.

Managers, in the end, must choose among these various opportunities, learn from their implementation, and initiate another high-payback item: training, faster computers, or new system software.

A static maintenance environment is a dead maintenance environment. Consider a U.S. steel industry that is dying for lack of investment in new technology. Software maintenance of your company's existing systems, if stagnant, can grow with each new system until it can literally break the corporation's back.

Good management depends on foresight. Start looking at ways to evolve toward a more productive and higher-quality software maintenance environment. Your focus may not take you to the moon, but you will be surprised how quickly you arrive at your goal.

Bibliography

Arthur, L. J. *Programmer Productivity*. Wiley, 1983.

Arthur, L. J. *Measuring Programmer Productivity and Software Quality*. Wiley, 1985.

Baker, A. L., S. Zweben. "A comparison of measures of control flow complexity." *IEEE Trans. Soft. Eng.* **7**(1), January 1981.

Boehm, B. A. "The high cost of software." Proceedings of the Symposium on High Cost Software. September 1973.

Boehm, B. A. *Software Engineering Economics*. Prentice-Hall, 1981.

Brooks, Frederick P. *The Mythical Man-Month*. Addison-Wesley, 1975.

Canning, R. G. "The maintenance iceberg." *EDP Analyzer* **10**(10), October 1972.

Capers Jones, T. *Programmer Productivity*. Prentice-Hall, 1985.

Cashman, P. M., and A. W. Holt. "A communications oriented approach to structuring the software maintenance environment." *Soft. Eng. Notes* **5**(1), January 1980, pp. 4–17.

Couger, J. D., and M. A. Colter. *Maintenance Programming*. Prentice-Hall, 1985.

Craig, G. R., et al. "Software Reliability Study." RADC–TR–74-250, TRW Corp., 1974.

DeRose, B., and T. Nyman. "The software life cycle—a management and technological challenge in the Department of Defense." *IEEE Trans. Soft. Eng.* **SE-4**(4), July 1978, pp. 309–318.

Kapur, G. "Reusable code in business." *ComputerWorld,* 1980.

Lipow, M. "Prediction of software failures." *J. Systems Software* **1**(1) December 1979. pp. 71–75.

Martin, James, and Carma McClure. *Software Maintenance: The Problem and It's Solutions*. Prentice-Hall, 1983.

McCabe, T. J. "A complexity measure." *IEEE Trans. Soft. Eng.* **2**(4), December 1980, pp. 308–320.

Mills, H. D. "Software development." *IEEE Trans. Soft. Eng.* **SE-2**(4), December 1976, pp. 265–273.

Myers, G. J. *Reliable Software through Composite Design.* Wiley, 1976.

Myers, G. J. *Software Testing.* Wiley, 1979.

Nolan, R. "Managing the crisis in data processing." *Harvard Bus. Rev.*, March–April 1979, pp. 115–126.

Parnas, D. L. "Designing Software for ease of extension and contraction." *IEEE Trans. Soft. Eng.*, 1979.

Peters, T. J. *A Passion for Excellence.* Random, 1985.

Pressman, R. S. *Software Engineering.* McGraw, 1982.

Weinberg, G. M. "Software maintenance." *Datalink,* May 14, 1979.

Zelkowitz, M. V. *Principles of Software Engineering and Design.* Prentice-Hall, 1979.

Index